The First Tube

Mike Horne and
Bob Bayman

UNDERGROUND

Capital Transport

First published 1990

ISBN 185414 128 7

Published in association with the Northern Line, London Underground Ltd
by Capital Transport Publishing, 38 Long Elmes, Harrow Weald, Middlesex

Printed by The KPC Group, Ashford, Kent

The authors and publisher would like to thank the following for their help during the preparation of this book: Doug Rose, David Sexton, Sheila Taylor and Anne Wilkinson.

The painting on the back cover of the Stockwell crossover as it would have appeared in locomotive days is by Printz Holman.

Many of the photographs are from the photographic archives of the London Transport Museum, 39 Wellington Street, London WC2, from whom copies are available for purchase.

The archer symbol shown opposite is used internally as the house symbol of the Northern Line. It is based upon Eric Aumonier's statue at East Finchley station, erected in 1939, and commemorates Finchley's ancient royal hunting connections. It has also been described as the arrow of rapid transit flying towards central London.

CONTENTS

PREFACE

On 4th November 1890 the City & South London Railway, a major component of what is now the Northern Line, was officially opened.

The achievement of the engineers who built this line cannot be over-emphasised. The line was both the first 'tube' railway and the first practical electric railway in the world. These were momentous achievements, being the beginning of what might now be regarded as a worldwide boom in the construction of 'Metro' systems.

It is the purpose of this book to explore the arrival of the City & South London Railway and to show how it developed to become an integral part of the Northern Line. As part of London's Underground we shall also look to the future of this pioneering line – towards the next hundred years.

London Before The Tubes

Today, the Greater London area occupies 610 square miles, and most of it is substantially built upon. But 150 years ago London was little bigger than the area presently enclosed within London Underground's Circle Line, which is a mere 6¾ square miles. It had taken several hundred years before that to expand from the walled City of London, only one square mile in size.

Although tiny by modern standards, the rapidly expanding London of 1840 was becoming big enough to present problems in communication. It must be borne in mind that both the telegraph and telephone were yet to be introduced (and the penny post had only just arrived that year). It had been as recently as 1829 when the first London 'omnibus' service began, though the proliferation of these horse-drawn vehicles did not by any means solve the growing transport problem, being inherently slow and contributing further to the congestion in the almost medieval streets.

Growth of London 1845/1880/1900. LUL

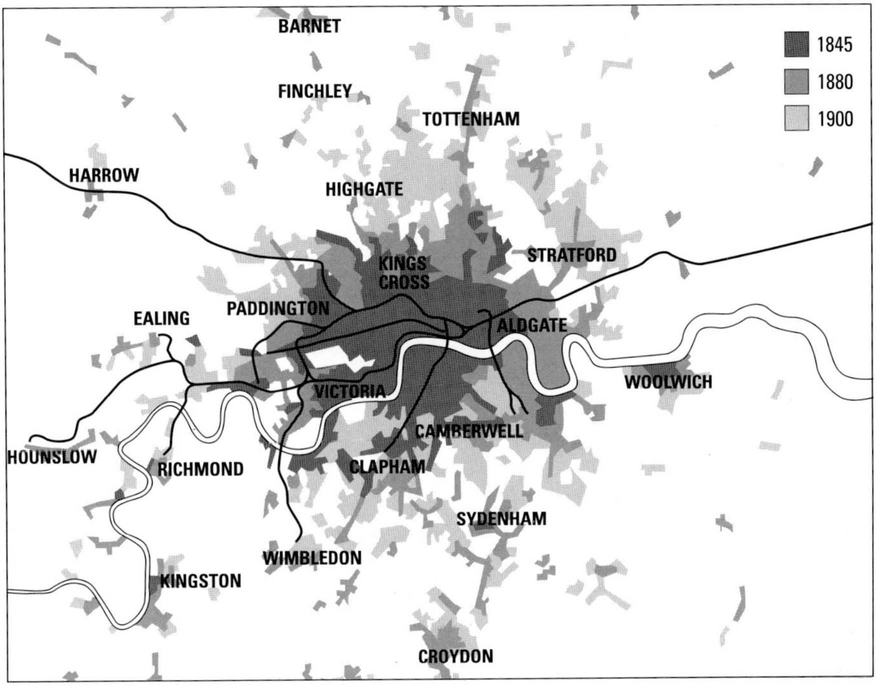

The arrival of the main line railways from the 1830s had further contributed to the mounting chaos, having been obliged to stop at London's outskirts, at Paddington, Euston and King's Cross, although those on the south and east were later to penetrate slightly further into the centre. Although the art of 'commuting' was virtually unknown, the arrival of the railways began to bring the Home Counties within easy reach of London, and a country home became a practical possibility – for so long as it remained country, of course.

Numerous schemes were proposed to ease the mounting problem. London was expanding at an increasing pace and the problems of travel were getting worse. After several years of argument it was agreed to build a railway beneath street level, connecting the main line termini together and bringing a railway into the City of London itself. This became the Metropolitan Railway and opened in 1863 from Paddington to Farringdon Street, via Edgware Road, Baker Street, Portland Road, Gower Street and King's Cross.

The Railway was a milestone in London's transport history. Although it was built to Brunel's broad gauge (7 feet) and used steam locomotion, it was novel in that much of it ran under the ground within tunnel (or, more strictly, a covered way). Construction was immensely disruptive. First a vast ditch had to be excavated, the walls of which were then lined with bricks. Then the roof had to be erected and the ground made good above. Although substantial demolition was required, the method of construction generally dictated that the line ran beneath the roadway, where the inconvenience caused to frontagers was considerable, and of course the road had temporarily to be stopped up while work took place.

By 1884 a completely circular underground railway had been built (now the Circle Line) and numerous extensions made into the emergent London Suburbs – though the extensions were almost all of the conventional type, either at or above ground level. The last links of this circle had cost a huge amount to finance and it was becoming clear that on grounds of both expense and inconvenience these shallow underground railways could never penetrate into modern central London. And so another answer had to be found.

Traffic congestion has kept road speed to around 10mph in central London since the 1850s. This scene, near the Royal Exchange at the turn of the century, shows why.
Guildhall Library

The answer came almost by chance – literally it was lateral thinking. At the same time as the Metropolitan Railway was being built an engineer named Barlow had been responsible for sinking cast iron cylinders into the Thames at Lambeth. Although these were to be part of the pier foundations for a suspension bridge (opened in 1862) it occurred to Barlow that were the cylinders to be laid horizontally it would be possible to connect them together and run what he described as an 'omnibus' through them beneath the ground. In succeeding years others were to develop the theme of pipes or tubes to a limited extent by digging a trench, inserting a pipe (or caisson) and covering it over. Only a small mail-conveying scheme (operated by pneumatic power) was in any way a success and two passenger carrying schemes failed come to fruition.

But Barlow pursued a different approach. He wanted to construct his iron-lined tunnels from beneath the ground. He adapted a concept used many years earlier by Sir Marc Brunel, that of using a massive shield at the working face to protect the workmen and to hold back the ground until the permanent tunnel had been erected. Barlow's shield was circular and was propelled forward by screw jacks, pushing against the completed tunnel behind. The tunnel rings had to be brought to site in a dismantled state in the form of segments which could be bolted together.

Barlow was first able to apply his invention in London, on a short subway beneath the Thames near the Tower of London. The subway was authorised by Act of Parliament in 1868 and opened in 1870. Initially it contained a cable-hauled car and the shafts at each end of the tunnel were equipped with lifts; passengers were conveyed at a small charge.

The venture was a commercial failure. In engineering terms, however, the scheme amply demonstrated the potential of this form of tunnelling. Two factors emerged. Firstly that a form of tunnelling now existed which was particularly well suited to the blue clay that exists as a fairly uniform stratum beneath much of London; this also permitted construction below many of the existing pipes and sewers of the City. Secondly, it was now possible to build a railway whose construction needed only a limited number of surface access shafts and entirely avoided the massive scale of disruption caused by the arrival of the Metropolitan Railway. London was now free to demand a railway more or less anywhere it was wanted.

The massive disruption caused while building the shallow covered ways was virtually unavoidable.
LT Museum

The Pioneer Tube

The engineering success of the Tower Subway encouraged Barlow to propose another, much larger, cross-river scheme in 1870 – the Southwark & City Subway which would have been about 1.3 miles long. Mindful, no doubt, of the financial results of the Tower Subway, backing was not forthcoming and the proposal was dropped. However continuing developments caused the idea to be revived a few years later, and in 1884 an Act of Parliament authorised the City & Southwark Subway between a point in the City near the Monument, and the Elephant & Castle, Southwark. Barlow was considerably aided by a former pupil of his, James Greathead, who designed the tunnelling shields required. Tunnelling started in 1886, but by the following year sufficient backing was available to support a southerly extension to Stockwell, and a further Act was passed.

Work began from a shaft sunk into the river at the Old Swan Pier, just upstream of London Bridge. Additional working shafts were built at intervals along the line of route. The tunnels were to be larger than those on the Tower Subway, at 10 feet 2 inches. This time the tunnelling shield was driven forward by means of hydraulic jacks, a method which has been adopted ever since. From the initial shaft in the river, twin tunnels were driven towards each terminus, one tunnel for each direction of traffic.

Greathead's original tunnelling shield. This design, with few modifications, has sufficed to create most of the running tunnels for the London Underground.
Proceedings of the Institution of Civil Engineers

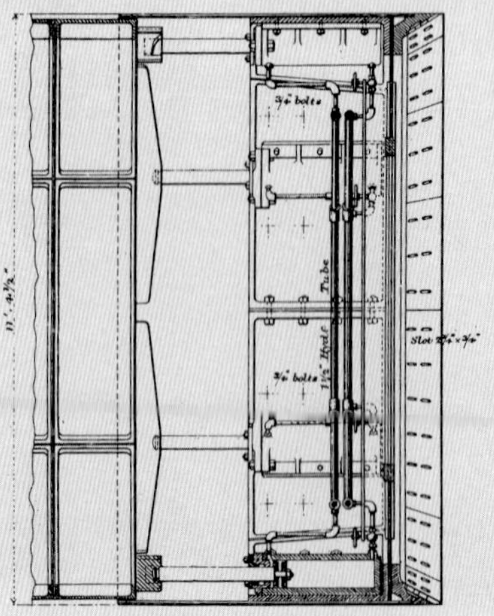

SECTION OF SHIELD.

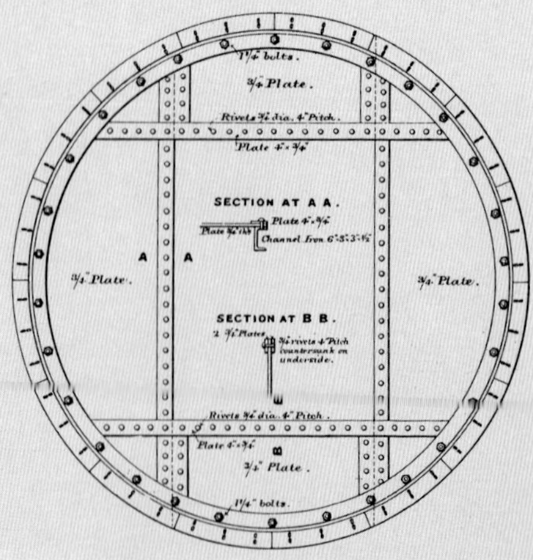

ELEVATION SHEWING CUTTER.

Stockwell Station, 4th November 1890, as the Prince of Wales arrives for the official opening and the first royal journey by tube railway. LT Museum

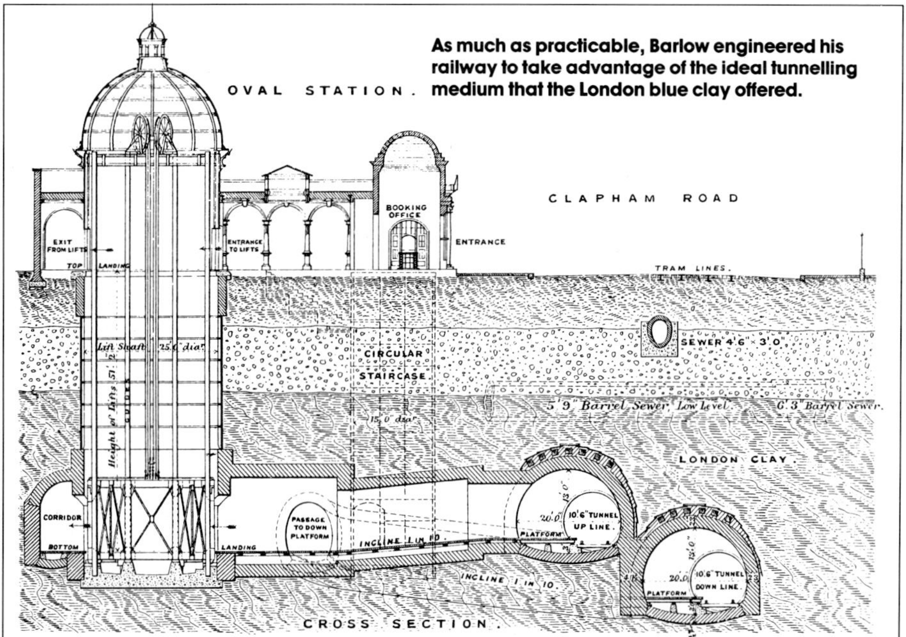

As much as practicable, Barlow engineered his railway to take advantage of the ideal tunnelling medium that the London blue clay offered.

Like the Tower Subway it was intended that the carriages be hauled by means of cable traction (which was by then in use on some tramways). This involved continuously driven cables to which the cars could clamp themselves by means of mechanical grippers controlled by the drivers. From 1888 the use of electric traction was considered as a means of overcoming some of the shortcomings of cables. It was a novel approach in view of the infancy of the industry but after successful experiments in 1889 the decision was made to adopt a three-rail electric traction system at 450 volts dc. This required the construction of a power station which at the time was among the largest in the world and the first built for dedicated railway use.

Two prototype electric locomotives were delivered and tested prior to the line's opening, using temporary generating plant at the Borough. One of these had the motors mounted directly on the axles while on the other the axles were driven via gearing. In the event the geared loco was rather noisy in operation and the remaining twelve locomotives were based on the first prototype. Signalling was of conventional railway pattern with signal cabins at each station using full-size mechanical lever frames. The signals themselves were semaphores, though in the running tunnels the restricted space meant that lamp signals were used.

The formal opening took place on 4th November 1890 and was performed by the Prince of Wales (subsequently King Edward VII) although public service did not begin until Thursday 18th December. By modern standards the railway was crude and primitive. By the standards of the day it was a leap into the future. The small electric locomotives were generally effective in hauling their three diminutive carriages at an acceptable speed and without the curse of the steam and smoke which pervaded the older Metropolitan and District Railways. The carriages provided adequate comfort even despite the lack of window space, not that there was much to look at. Access was gained from the ends, where gated gangways gave access to station platforms.

C&SLR Carriage No.30. The short wheelbase and the long bogie frames carrying the separate gated entrance vestibule are clearly seen. The very small windows, and the cushioned interior of the carriages, gave rise to the nickname of 'Padded Cells'. This carriage is now at the LT Museum. LT Museum

One of the original C&SLR Locomotives, No.10, in later modified form outside Stockwell depot. The piping on the roof carries the air brake across to the adjacent carriage. LT Museum

1897 and King William Street station is decorated for Queen Victoria's Diamond Jubilee. Beneath the flags a notice proclaims 'To the Oval in Ten Minutes' — a time unmatched by the traffic-encumbered horse-bus.
Guildhall Library

Like the modern Victoria Line, the City & South London Railway (as it had become just before opening) was entirely underground except for the depot, which was reached by a very steep gradient near Stockwell station. In fact this was worked by cable traction. The power station was on the depot site and hydraulic pressure was also created here and conveyed to the stations for operation of the hydraulic station lifts. Each intermediate station (Borough, Elephant & Castle, Kennington and Oval) had a separate platform for each track. At the City station (called King William Street) there was a single track with a platform each side while at Stockwell there was a single platform with a track each side. Although the running tunnels were of cast iron and circular, the 200ft long station platforms were of brick and the lower portion was flattened off, to avoid wasted space.

As a deep level tube railway the City & South London was an engineering success. As an electric railway, it was a triumph too. There *were* problems. The brick station construction led to some subsidence (and was not repeated) and the electricity upset some delicate measurements at Greenwich Observatory, some five miles away. But these were trivial problems compared with the arrival of a clean, new and, above all, successful new system of transportation which was to transform travel patterns in London over the next century.

The City & South London Grows

One of the main constraints on the C&SLR was that of being a pioneer in the field. In particular the layout at the north end of the line, set out for cable operation, was not satisfactory, nor did the alignment lend itself to future expansion. In 1895 the layout of King William Street was altered to give a twin track arrangement with an island platform between, though this did further restrict possible train lengths. Services were gradually improved, requiring additional locomotives and carriages, enhanced signalling and increased capacity at the generating station.

Plans were made for a northerly extension, but in order to achieve a satisfactory arrangement the brave decision was made to abandon the near mile-long section from King William Street to a point just north of Borough, and to build a new stretch of railway in substitute. Parliamentary powers were obtained for the extension of the line to Islington in 1893, and included the diversion from Borough. Stations were to be constructed at London Bridge, Bank, Moorgate, Old Street, City Road and Angel. The line opened as far as Moorgate in 1900 and Angel in 1901.

The removal of the King William Street bottleneck at last allowed of a modest southerly extension too. Powers had been obtained for this as long previously as 1890, but it was feared that without an increase in capacity further north the line would not be able to cope. Extension work began in 1898 and the new route opened in 1900 with stations at Clapham Road (now Clapham North) and Clapham Common. This extension required much improved arrangements at Stockwell including slight enlargement at the depot, the substitution of a carriage lift for the former incline and the construction of additional sidings at low level.

At Angel, Clapham Road and Clapham Common there were island platforms enclosed within a single 30ft diameter tunnel. At the other stations there were separate tunnels for each platform; all platform tunnels were now circular and built of cast iron. Electric lifts were provided taking passengers to street level buildings, except at Bank where, uniquely among railway stations, the booking hall was built within the crypt of a church. Interchange was available at Bank with the Central London Railway, and at Moorgate with the Metropolitan Railway.

The enlarged line demanded considerably improved power supply arrangements in replacement for the primitive (and barely adequate) equipment provided at the opening. In the event a completely new power station was provided (also at Stockwell depot) accompanied by a 5-wire direct current distribution system which included boosters and storage batteries at other locations. The traction voltage was increased to 500 Volts.

In 1907 the C&SLR made its final expansion while still an independent company and reached Euston, with an intermediate station at King's Cross. At platform level Euston was very much like Angel, being accommodated in a single tunnel, whilst at street level there was an ornate station building in Eversholt Street.

Opposite **The surface buildings of the C&SLR's Euston station opened in 1907 and closed in 1914. The Charing Cross, Euston & Hampstead Railway surface buildings also closed, concentrating passengers into the shared booking office and lifts beneath the LNWR main line station — an arrangement which at times caused considerable congestion.** LT Museum

Left **With a platform 40ft by 10ft and rated for loads of up to 16 tons, the Stockwell Carriage lift could convey either locomotives or carriages the sixty feet from surface to tunnel level.**
M.A.C. Horne Collection

At King's Cross there were separate tunnels with the station lifts coming down between the platforms. At top level there was a ticket hall beneath the forecourt of King's Cross, but with a subway leading to St Pancras station. Between Angel and King's Cross a signal cabin was provided at Weston Street, to shorten an otherwise long section.

Even before the new extensions it was necessary to enhance services and provide additional carriages and locomotives. These additional carriages had been delivered with slightly larger windows. The extensions required substantially more rolling stock and the locomotives were of a more powerful type, built by Cromptons. This time carriages, though still cramped, were very much more plush and had more or less full-sized windows. In addition some of the earliest stock was modernised. In due course 5-coach trains became the standard. Considerable modifications were required to the signalling. Although it remained mechanically operated, numerous additional 'home' signals were added to improve capacity.

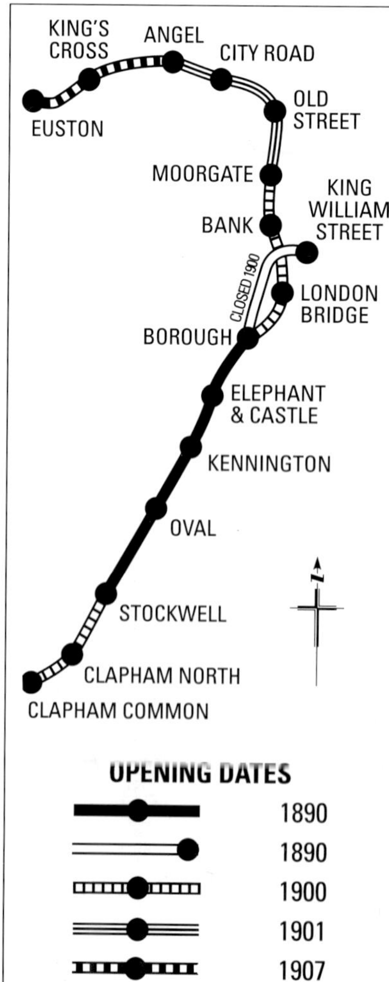

Left **Map showing C&SLRly opening dates (modern names used for clarity).** LUL

Below **Moorgate station in 1914. The company was quick to take advantage of the prime sites occupied by their central London stations and built lucrative office space above. This building became the headquarters of the C&SLR.** LT Museum

With the abandonment of the former City terminus it became possible to operate four-car trains. The additional rolling stock this required was built by several manufacturers, these cars being constructed by G. F. Milnes & Company. The design was a modified version of the original stock. M.A.C. Horne Collection

C&SLR crest, as carried on the reverser key of the train used for the ceremonial opening of the Morden extension in 1926. LT Museum

The Hampstead Tube

The technical success of the City & South London Railway soon caused a number of schemes to be put forward for further tube railways in London. One of these emerged in 1893, and was called the Charing Cross, Euston & Hampstead Railway. This would have run from a site in the Strand to Hampstead, with a branch line proposed from Warren Street to King's Cross via Euston. The main line would have run under Charing Cross, Tottenham Court and Hampstead Roads, and thence beneath Haverstock Hill.

In common with many tube schemes the construction of the line was characterised by years of delay while the question of finance was settled. During this time the proposed route was adjusted such that Euston was incorporated on the main line (and King's Cross dropped) and a branch was proposed from Camden Town to Tufnell Park (later Highgate but then cut back to Archway). Even by the turn of the century the money had not been found, though the Scheme (for which powers were obtained) had been kept alive.

In the end it was an American syndicate which procured the money and built the line. Under the control of one Charles Tyson Yerkes a company had been formed to electrify the steam operated Metropolitan District Railway. When the CCEHR's interests were acquired the electrification company was re-established as the 'Underground Electric Railways Company of London Ltd' and became a holding company for this scheme, together with others (the UERL continued to operate much of London's transport until 1933). With capital at last, the construction of the CCEHR could begin, and work started in 1903.

The line opened on 22nd June 1907 with trains running from Charing Cross to both Highgate and Hampstead, with some trains projected to Golders Green where the depot was located. Trains were operated on the multiple-unit system (that is, without separate locomotives). Three types of car were built: those with motors (which also had a driving cab), and those without motors (half of which had driving cabs). The cars were built in America but shipped here in a dismantled state and erected in Manchester.

A view of the track outside Golders Green station, looking towards the tunnel mouth, prior to opening. In this open section signalling is by pneumatically controlled lower quadrant semaphore signals. LT Museum

HAMPSTEAD HEATH
NANCY SMITH
THE NEAREST POINT TO LONDON
FOR FUN AND FRESH AIR
BY
UNDERGROUND
SPOTTISWOODE & Cº Lᵀᴰ LITHO, 5 NEW STREET SQUARE, LONDON, E.C.

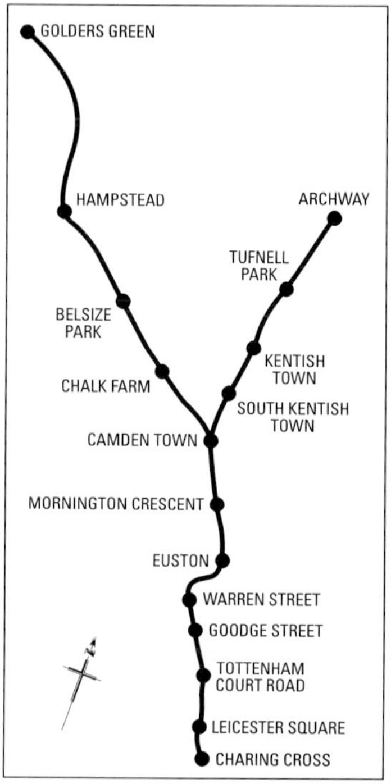
GOLDERS GREEN
HAMPSTEAD
ARCHWAY
TUFNELL PARK
BELSIZE PARK
KENTISH TOWN
CHALK FARM
SOUTH KENTISH TOWN
CAMDEN TOWN
MORNINGTON CRESCENT
EUSTON
WARREN STREET
GOODGE STREET
TOTTENHAM COURT ROAD
LEICESTER SQUARE
CHARING CROSS

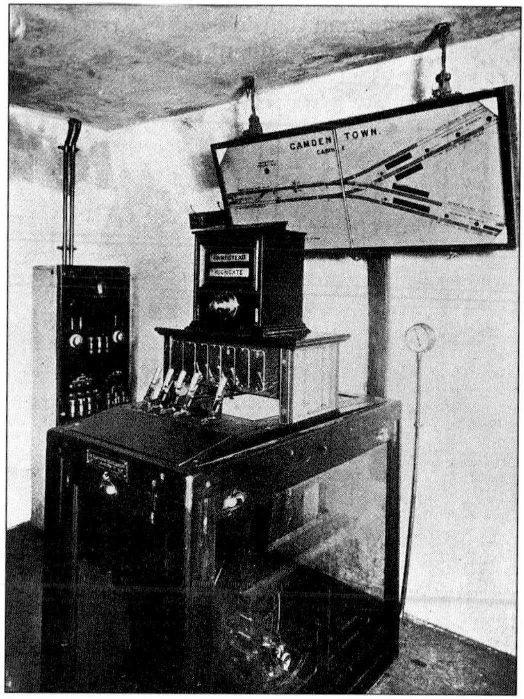
CAMDEN TOWN.
HAMPSTEAD
HIGHGATE

Stations were built to an essentially standard design, being steel-framed and clad in a ruby-red glazed tilework. They were of two storeys, with the upper floor used for the electric lift machinery and staff accommodation. At platform level the platforms could take trains up to seven cars long and had tiled walls embodying a coloured pattern. At Oxford Street and Charing Cross there were no station buildings and the booking halls were built beneath the street and main line station forecourt respectively.

Power was taken from a generating station on the Thames near Chelsea, which also supplied the District Railway and two other tube lines which were owned by the same holding company. Four substations were provided, one shared with the District. Interchange was provided at Leicester Square and Oxford Street with east-west tube lines, and at Euston with the City & South London (although a separate surface station was built, there was also access to the ticket hall beneath the main line station used jointly with the C&SLR).

Little changed for the first few years except some station renaming (thus Euston Road became Warren Street, Tottenham Court Road became Goodge Street, and Oxford Street became Tottenham Court Road). The first extension was a projection of the line southwards from Charing Cross (which became 'Strand' station) to the District Line's station at Charing Cross. Although this was rather less than a quarter of a mile away the considerably improved interchange was felt to be worthwhile. The extension opened in 1914 in the form of a single track reversing loop, thus only one new platform was needed. The platform was sharply curved (being a part of the loop) and exists today as the northbound platform at what is now Embankment station.

The provision of a reversing loop introduced a problem which has remained with the line and its successors ever since. The carriages were delivered with the electrical inter-car jumpers and air hoses arranged on the assumption that the cars would never be turned round (which would put the jumpers on the wrong side). The loop meant that trains were frequently running 'wrong way round', thereby rendering them unable to couple properly with unturned stock. A minor problem, it may be thought, but one where the existence of cars which could not easily couple to others created a maintenance problem (more spares were needed) as well as operating difficulties in an emergency. In later years a turntable had to be installed at Golders Green in an attempt to ease the difficulty.

Interestingly, the Hampstead tube was the first to embody a tube junction and branches. This immediately created a need for passengers south of Camden Town to know where the northward-bound trains were going. Since the carriages were gate-ended there were plenty of staff to call the information out, but the trains also carried destination signs on the leading car. A system of coloured lights was also used. To warn the signalman at Camden Town of the correct destination of trains, plungers were installed at Mornington Crescent which northbound drivers had to operate.

Facing Page Top Left **The Charing Cross, Euston & Hampstead Railway as opened in 1907 (modern names used for clarity).** LUL

Facing Page Top Right **The simple interior of Camden Town signal cabin with the small five lever (plus two unused) electro-pneumatic signal frame.** LT Museum

Facing Page Bottom **Part of Camden Town junction after reconstruction in 1924 showing northbound tunnels; the left tunnel is from Charing Cross towards Highgate, the centre one from the City to Highgate & Golders Green and the right tunnel is from Charing Cross to Golders Green.** LT Museum

Far Left
A day at the Zoo? Camden Town, Hampstead Tube.
LT Museum

Left
Original ticket window, Hampstead station.
Andrew Bronn

Mornington Crescent station typifies the house style adopted by the CCE&HR for its 1907 station buildings.
Capital Transport

Below **Tile frieze from original CCE&HR Euston platform.**
Doug Rose

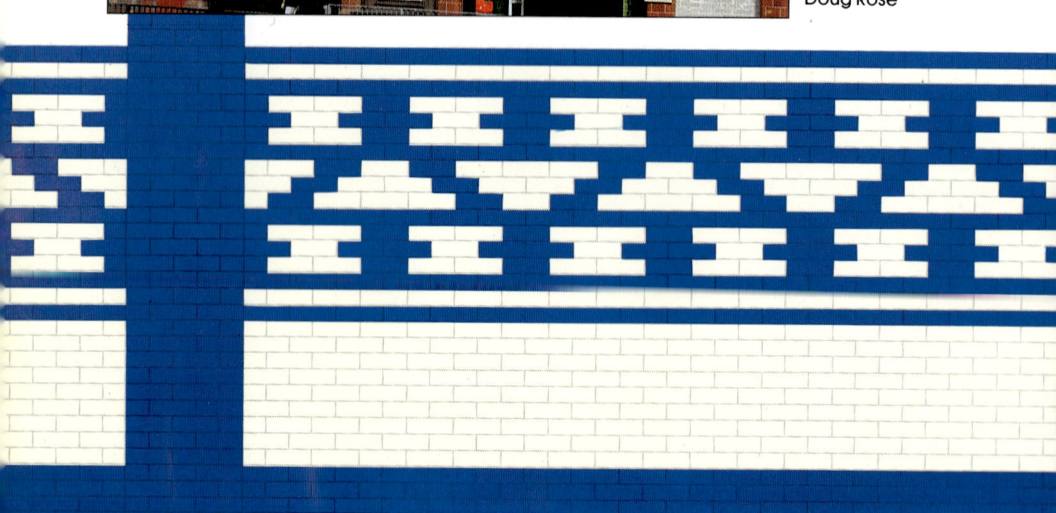

The 1907 ACF 'gate' stock was the first multiple unit stock used on the Northern Line. Operated as five-car trains in busy periods, the sets were uncoupled to allow two-car sets to operate at quiet times. The leather strap-hangers suggest that, unlike the C&SLR, the CCE&HR was prepared for rush hour traffic from the outset. LT Museum

Golders Green station forecourt. The tree growing through the canopy was encased when the sheltered area was extended and it survived in this form for some years.

Golders Green station and depot, although in the open country initially, were designed for handling extensive traffic should the opportunity arise. Hence the provision of four platform faces — the centre pair for departure and the outer faces for arrivals. M.A.C. Horne Collection

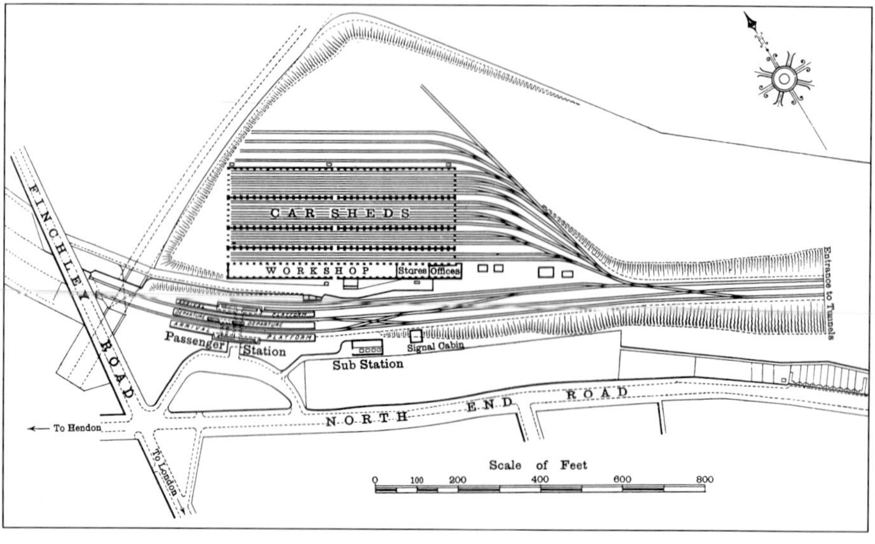

The Northern Line Emerges

Even while the CCEHR was on the drawing board there were plans for another railway, the Edgware and Hampstead, which proposed to build a line between those two places. The E & H obtained an Act of Parliament in 1902 but the usual financial problems ensued. After some negotiation the company was absorbed by the Underground Group which proposed an end-on connection at Golders Green with the CCEHR. Yet another company (the Watford & Edgware) proposed to build a line from Watford, via Aldenham to Edgware, where it would meet the E&HR end on, and an Act of Parliament was obtained in 1903. In this form the scheme did not materialise, despite some land acquisition.

In 1910 the CCEHR became part of the London Electric Railway (an amalgam of three UERL tube lines) and became known as the LER's 'Hampstead' line. The LER then acquired the Edgware & Hampstead company and proposed to begin work in 1912, the railway becoming in effect an northward extension of the Hampstead line through mainly unspoilt countryside to Edgware, considerable housing development being anticipated. By this time the route between Golders Green and Hendon had been modified, a better route northwards through rapidly developing Golders Green being necessary. Although land acquisition had started, the First World War effectively put a stop to the extension, and work did not resume until 1921. The extension opened northwards to Brent and Hendon in November 1923. The further projection via

Summer 1923, and the station platform at Hendon begins to take shape amidst the fields.
LT Museum

Colindale and Burnt Oak to Edgware did not open until the following year (although Burnt Oak opened a little later). Construction was almost entirely in open air with stations consisting of island platforms linked to station buildings faced in imposing Portland stone with doric columns (except at Burnt Oak where a temporary building was erected). A short section of line just north of Hendon pierced high ground by means of twin tube tunnels. The extension was the first on the Underground to use coloured light signals in the open sections.

In 1913 the City & South London Railway had been purchased by the Underground Group and had, so far as possible, been integrated with the rest of the Underground. There was, however, no possibility of full integration while the C&SLR still operated its antiquated equipment and rolling stock which, though none of it was more than 23 years old, was outdated by prevailing standards, such had been the rate of progress elsewhere. Various schemes were looked at, the major problem being the short platforms and restrictive diameter of the tunnels – 10ft 2in ruling diameter compared with about 11ft 8in on more recent systems. It was rapidly decided that platform extension and tunnel enlargement would be the only answer, and this would be coupled with a link with the Hampstead Line at Camden Town which would make use of the capacity available on the northern branches and provide a through route from the north to the City.

Facing Page **A Fred Taylor poster illustrating, with some artistic licence, housebuilding around the newly-completed Brent station, opened in 1923.** LT Museum

Left **A 1924 poster encouraging people to move out of inner London to commute by Underground from the countryside. It was not of course very long before scenes not unlike that in the upper part of the poster had moved to Edgware also.** LT Museum

Below **Workmen put the finishing touches to Brent station's island platform.** LT Museum

During reconstruction at Borough and Kennington stations, temporary sidings for engineers' trains were installed on the former platform sites. LT Museum

Some extent of the urgency with which reconstruction was felt needed may be gauged by the hope that work would start as soon as the necessary powers had been obtained (which was in 1914). Again the First World War intervened and work could not begin until 1922. A valiant effort was made to try to keep the C&SLR operating whilst the immense task of reconstruction took place. Nevertheless the section north of Moorgate was closed from 9th August 1922 as the nature of the work required it. In due course Kennington and Borough stations temporarily closed and became working sites, and some areas of the line had to be worked single track (the traffic day along the whole route was much shortened too). An auxiliary bus service therefore operated along the route to ease the load.

In November 1923 a serious subsidence near the Borough closed the line down completely, and it was subsequently decided to withdraw the train service entirely until reconstruction was complete. The bus service was strengthened during this period.

The line reopened between Euston and Moorgate on 20th April 1924 and this included the new link between Camden Town and Euston (C&SLR). Through trains began to operate immediately. The remainder of the C&SLR, between Moorgate and Clapham Common, reopened on 1st December 1924. One station, City Road, was not reconstructed as the light traffic did not justify it. It closed permanently in 1922.

The much improved capacity of the C&SLR following reconstruction meant that extension could be contemplated southwards from Clapham Common into the open fields of Surrey, near Morden, via busy Balham and Tooting. Powers were obtained in 1923 and these also allowed for a link between Kennington and Charing Cross, thus offering a choice of central London destinations for those living south of the river. This would require high capacity junction work at Kennington only marginally less complicated than that which was about to come into service at Camden Town.

To assess the suitability of the station designs for the Morden Extension, the LER constructed a full-size entrance mock-up in an exhibition hall. LT Museum

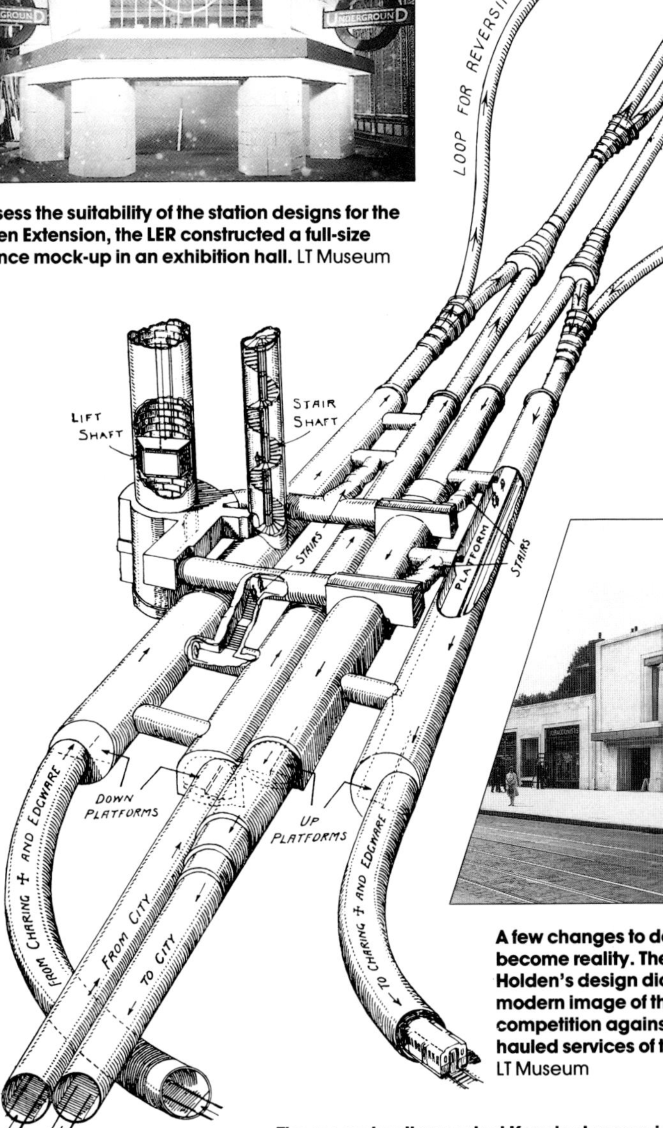

A few changes to detail and the mock-up has become reality. The strikingly clean lines of Holden's design did much to project the modern image of the Underground in its competition against the still largely steam-hauled services of the Southern Railway. LT Museum

The reconstruction work at Kennington required the provision of a reversing loop, a siding and two new flanking platforms as well as the transposition of one of the running lines with an existing platform. M.A.C. Horne Collection

Work began in earnest on the Morden extension early in 1924, while that for the Kennington – Charing Cross link began in April the same year. Progress was rapid and both new lines were opened on 13th September 1926, though not all work was quite complete and Balham station opened only in December.

South of Strand station the new southbound line diverged from the loop to pass through a new platform at Charing Cross – the northbound line diverged south of the existing platform. Twin tubes continued through new platforms at Waterloo (where the Bakerloo Line station was enlarged and provided with escalators). The tubes continued to Kennington where new platforms flanked the old City & South London station. South of here running connections were made with the C&SLR while for a proportion of the Hampstead Line's service a new reversing loop was constructed.

South of Clapham Common twin tubes ran most of the way to Morden and new stations were opened at Clapham South, Balham, Trinity Road, Tooting Broadway, Colliers Wood and South Wimbledon. Morden was built as an open air station with three tracks and five platforms. Beyond the station the line continued into a new depot, primarily arranged for stabling sidings with limited repair and maintenance facilities.

The new stations were all built in a similar style, much influenced by the architectural style of Charles Holden and making considerable use of Portland stone facing. At platform level, stations had individual platforms for each direction of travel and escalators came down to a concourse between them (usually the escalators carried people directly to street level). The C&SLR reconstructed stations were modernised to look similar in style where possible, and in many cases escalators were installed to replace the earlier lifts – though adapting existing stations rarely produced an ideal result.

Platforms on the Morden extension stations were similar in design, being clad in the then 'house style' of white and green glazed tiles. Andrew Bronn

Facing Page **Poster proclaiming the achievement of the rebuilding of the City & South London Railway; the Northern Line as we now know it had substantially taken shape.**

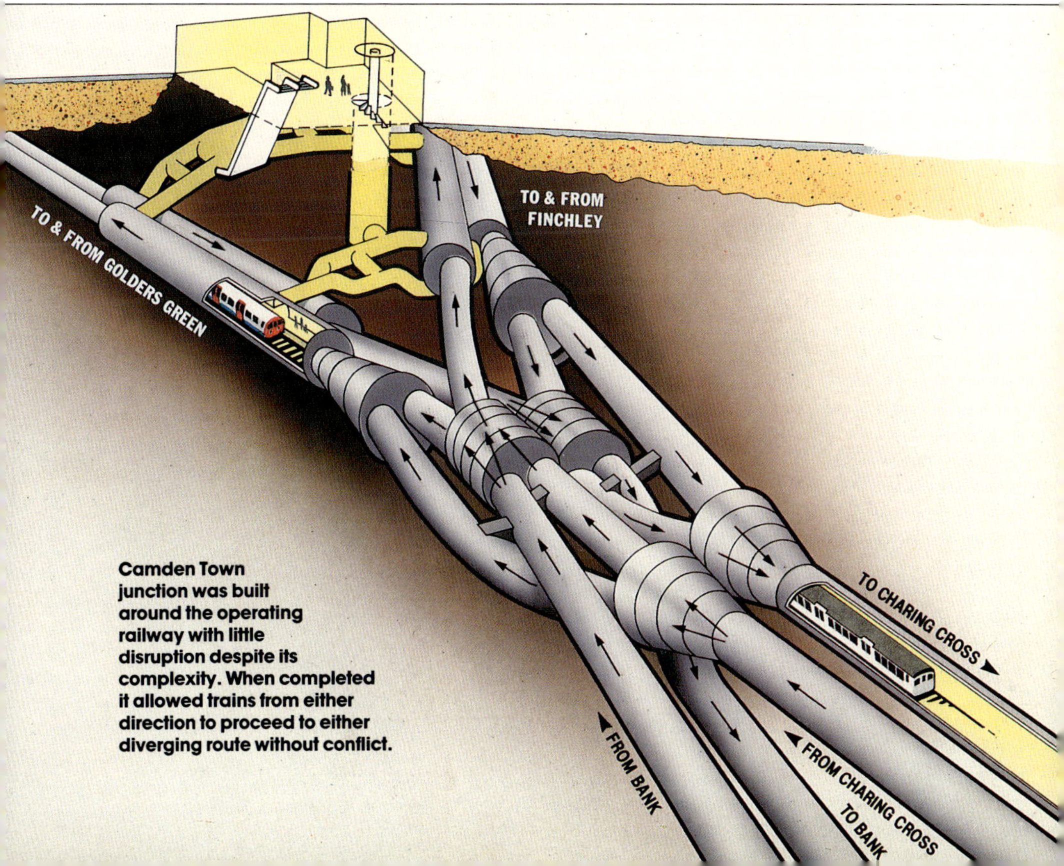

Camden Town junction was built around the operating railway with little disruption despite its complexity. When completed it allowed trains from either direction to proceed to either diverging route without conflict.

A car of the rolling stock purchased for the extensions of 1923-1926 and for replacement of earlier stock. F. Moore

To service the new extensions and to replace the antiquated C&SLR locomotives and carriages, a substantial order was placed for new rolling stock. Following some experimental cars delivered in 1922 orders were placed for successive batches of new cars of all-steel construction and fitted with air doors (allowing a reduction in trainstaff to a driver and two guards per train – a few years later only one guard was provided). Most of this stock arrived between 1923 and 1926 but later batches of similar stock allowed the old Hampstead line's gate-ended cars to be scrapped (achieved by 1930). Trains were generally of 6-car or 7-car lengths, the latter eventually becoming standard. Off-peak, 3-or 4-car trains were run.

The complex new services created an urgent need for equipment to describe for the passenger's benefit both the destination and routeing of the trains. This equipment already existed at signal cabins (the signalmen only rarely being able to see the trains) and the apparatus was extended to the majority of stations, information being displayed on platforms by means of illuminated glass signs (only recently superseded). Initially the new trains carried above the cab door a roller blind with the destinations on it, and beneath this was a swivelling plate showing the route. In later batches of stock the information was given by destination plates displayed below the offside cab window, the earlier cars being modified to suit.

Although both the LER and the C&SLR continued separate legal existences, the conglomeration resulting from the new junctions and through services meant that the companies had no option but to function as a single operational railway. With a route from Morden to Kennington, thence two possible routes to Euston and Camden Town, and two northern branches (to Edgware or Highgate), it is clear that by 1926 the basis of the present day Northern Line already existed. In fact the name Northern Line was not coined until 1937 and in the meantime such less than satisfactory names as 'Hampstead & City Line' and 'Edgware-Morden Line' had to suffice.

The Northern and its Suburbs

For 150 years London's development has been linked directly with some form of transport – frequently to railways and trams; occasionally to road networks. The first tube lines were constructed almost entirely to profit from existing heavily used transport corridors, although in the case of the City & South London Railway development was still occurring at the south end of the line as it carried its first passengers.

In 1907 the Hampstead tube quite literally broke new ground in opening to a rural crossroads at Golders Green, then beyond the London built-up area with a population density of only 8-10 persons per acre. The railway needed to get this far for depot space, but there was also clear intent to benefit from traffic generated by developing the existing fields within easy reach of the station – and thus of central London.

This development was, it turned out, successful beyond the developers' wildest dreams and the resultant building boom showed that the provision of good public transport was very much a dynamic process. Within a couple of decades the fields had entirely disappeared beneath densely packed streets of quite large and expensive houses – houses of a much more modern design than the terraces previously associated with London rail corridors. The growth was, in fact, so rapid that it nearly thwarted plans for the northward extension of the line from Golders Green station, which ultimately proceeded only by the demolition of a number of new houses and cutting of some roads (which can be clearly seen now). Many of the new residents became long-term tube travellers and paid back the railway handsomely. The first tube suburb had been born.

So began a partnership which was to last right through the 1920s and 1930s: the Underground brought areas to life as new suburbs, which were then interdependent with the railway. The construction of the Edgware branch, opened in 1924, was almost entirely across undeveloped land, although this state of affairs was not to last long. The Morden extension, by contrast, was substantially through densely packed residential districts but the terminus itself was indeed in virgin countryside. The Barnet line, then

Built on what was then the edge of Edgware village, Edgware station was planned as a railhead, with integrated bus feeder services biting deep into the catchment areas of the neighbouring Metropolitan, LNE and LM&S Railways
LT Museum

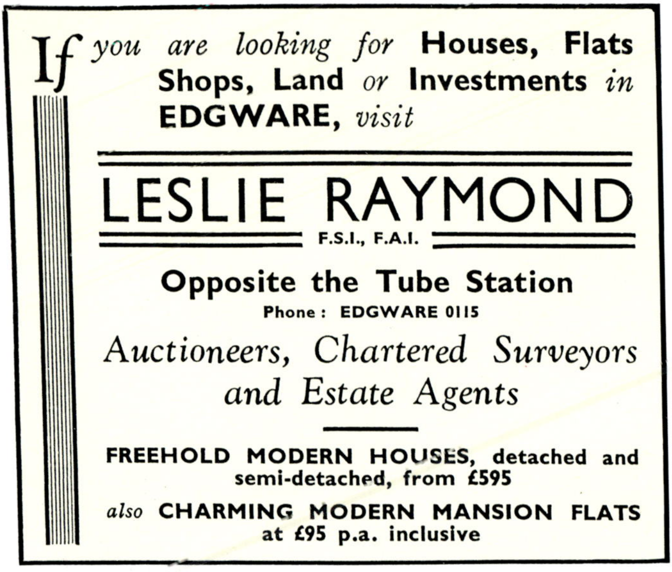

An estate agent's advertisement, noting the proximity of his office to the 'tube', from an Underground Timetable of 1934. Walter Leslie Raymond was son of a Golders Green dairyman (one of the few inhabitants of the area prior to 1907) and his career as an estate agent improved in fortune dramatically from profits made during the urbanisation of Golders Green. Raymond moved to Edgware shortly before the railway opened and was responsible (among others) for substantial development within the area.

Suburban London would have spread further but for post-war planning legislation following on from the 1938 Green Belt Act. The 1935-40 New Works Programme, of which more is written in the next chapter, included three new stations north of Edgware. Elstree South would have looked like this; a statue of a Roman centurion is mounted on the roof. R.E. Bayman Collection

Stations on the Edgware branch consisted of a single island platform accessed by a footbridge or a subway from the booking hall, the latter being at road level. A sign above the platform name reads 'Alight Here for Stag Lane Aerodrome' — a neighbouring aerodrome to Hendon, which was built over by developers in the early 1930s. LT Museum

still a relatively infrequent LNER steam branch, had already established itself as a lifeline to the isolated communities through Finchley, which had begun sprouting cottages and villas from Victorian times. Development here was more sedate, but by the end of the 1930s the combined efforts of the 'Met' tramway, the railway and the orbital North Circular Road had joined Barnet and Finchley to London.

Architecturally, the Underground was often seen as a leader in the communities served. The stations on the Edgware branch, designed by S.A. Heaps, rapidly became the focus of local development and were entirely in keeping with the spread of shopping parades and semis radiating outwards, emphasising the role of the railway as an integral part of the new suburb. Charles Holden was appointed architect for the Morden extension. Here the emphasis was changed to make the stations stand out in the street – indeed when the line was opened in 1926 searchlights were mounted on them – and to offer a wide, well-lit and welcoming shop window to the local residents. This technique was developed and perfected over the next few years: combined with the company's drive for attention to detail and sense of completeness it resulted in some designs achieving world-wide acclaim. On the Northern Line, the present-day Highgate and East Finchley stations ably demonstrate the ultimate pre-war stage of this development, although sadly the former has never reached completion itself.

The Barnet branch to this day is an exception to this rule. At the time of the great suburban spread it was still operated by infrequent and relatively slow steam trains. Its stations mostly occupied back-street sites and, having been robustly built in early Victorian times, did not generally require reconstruction to handle the steady rise in traffic. Most of the stations conformed very much with our thoughts today of sleepy semi-rural branches, with coal yards, sidings and little signal boxes. The London and North Eastern Railway, successor here to the Great Northern, kept its attention firmly on what we would now regard as inter-city traffic and paid scant regard to the needs of London commuters. The trains themselves often became delayed on the congested sections between Finsbury Park and various London termini (King's Cross, Moorgate and Broad Street were all used). One technique used to regain lost time was to non-stop stations in the down direction on the way to High Barnet in the morning peak, acknowledging the light demand in that direction. Given the irregular spacing of the trains – seldom more frequent than every 20 minutes – this was singularly unhelpful for those who did depend on the service. In the 1920s one irate father wrote to the company complaining that his daughter was thus stranded on her way to Queen Elizabeth's Girls Grammar School at High Barnet, pointing out that Woodside Park was a miserable place to wait on a winter's morning. The railway did nothing about the train service but they did instruct the stationmaster to provide a fire in the waiting room!

To be fair the LNER did make some response to the pressures of suburban development in the Finchley area in agreeing to provide a new station at Nether Street, between Church End (now Finchley Central) and Woodside Park, in 1933. "New" is perhaps not quite the correct description, since as a result of the company's lack of funds the station was almost entirely second-hand. Booking office, waiting rooms and footbridge all came from various locations in northern England bringing to Finchley a station which did not begin to match the masterpieces then being opened on the nearby Southgate extension of the Piccadilly Line. This little station did not have much luck in naming either – elsewhere developers were to add names like Oakwood and Albany Park to the London map, but here the local estate agents could come up with nothing more inspired than "West Finchley". The station actually lies to the north east of the equally ineptly named Finchley Central.

Despite the seemingly cavalier attitude of the main line company towards this local branch, the railway had spotted the possibilities of developing this traffic much earlier. In 1906 the Great Northern published a booklet which, under a heading "Exchange fog for sunshine" pointed out the rent and tax advantages of the suburbs, observing: "The neighbourhood of Finchley is charmingly wooded, and on every site tall elms and silver beeches form picturesque backgrounds to delightful views. The district is exceedingly healthy, the average yearly death rate being only about nine per thousand". This theme was to be repeated throughout London's suburbs until war stopped play in 1939, and was widely used to attract families from the inner city to the clean new suburbs. Catch phrases such as "Live where? – Edgware!" became almost the norm and were widely used in advertising. Certainly, access to the tube gave benefits which agents and speculative builders readily drew attention to.

Laing was a prolific builder of relatively highly specified houses in north west London, and in 1939 advertised its Edgware estate as being 8 minutes from the Edgware stations (there was still an LNER one then), although one is tempted to ponder the form of transport used to gauge this time! Earlier, Laing had advertised its Queensbury Estate "5 minutes walk from Burnt Oak tube", only later mentioning that "Queensbury Met. Station" was "actually on site". The roots of this apparent oddity were almost certainly the high main-line fare scales originally charged by the Metropolitan on its Stanmore extension (today's Jubilee Line) and its circuitous route to town compared with the Edgware Tube.

Facing Page **Indicating the trend away from traditional rented accommodation, this Laings advertisement emphasises the convenience of the Tube Station — a major selling point — and stresses the low cost leaseholds on their new houses, promoting the dream of a verdant health-giving suburbia.** R.E. Bayman Collection

"Mardale Drive" on Laings Springfield Estate

SPRINGFIELD GARDEN SUBURB

Edgware Road and Kingsbury Road

COLINDALE, N.W.9

MANY parts of Laings Springfield Garden Suburb are as high as Hampstead Heath and have the same bracing health-giving atmosphere and open views. Yet there are a number of sites where little or no hill climbing is necessary.

The suburb stands on the main Edgware Road with its frequent service of buses, trams and the Colindale Tube Station only a few minutes walk away.

Several schools practically adjoin the Estate and plans are in hand for a new school on the Estate itself; shopping parades also adjoin the houses.

To preserve the amenities of the Estate a 999 years lease has been arranged.

HOW TO GET THERE.—Hampstead Tube to Colindale Station, thence a few minutes walk. By alighting at Hendon Central Station, Bus Nos. 83 or 183 will put you down within one minute of the Estate Office. Buses 142, 83 and 183 pass the Estate.

Telephone : COLINDALE 6664

PRICES AT SPRINGFIELD GARDEN SUBURB

Semi-Detached Type	Price 999 yrs. Lease	Deposit	WEEKLY OUTGOINGS (Approximately)			
			To Building Society	Ground Rent	Rates	TOTAL
'R.A.'	£650	£50	18/7	2/4 (£6)	4/11	25/10
'A'	£699	£50	20/2	2/8 (£7)	5/4	28/2
'B'	£780	£60	22/4	3/- (£8)	6/-	31/4
'G'	£725	£50	20/11	2/8 (£7)	5/9	29/4
'E'	£880	£70	25/5	3/- (£8)	7/2	35/7

For Accommodation and Room Sizes see page 17.

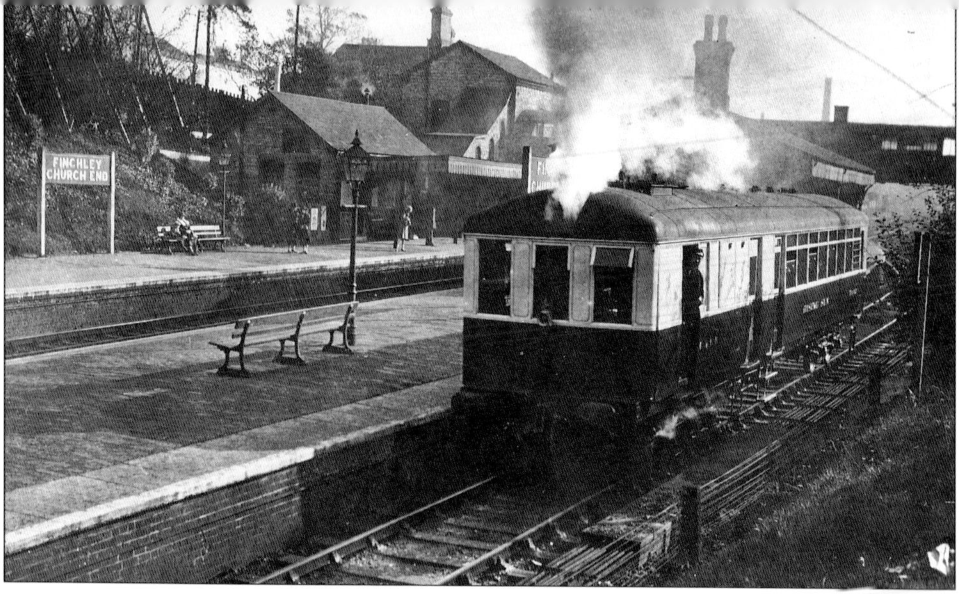

LNER Sentinel steam railcar No.51912 leaves Finchley Church End (now Finchley Central) for Edgware in October 1929 during a period of trial running on the service. Designed for low-cost operation on rural routes, these vehicles were less successful in the London area where they compared unfavourably with electric trains, trams and motor buses. Hulton

In the same area Hilbery Chaplin was advertising its Stag Lane Aerodrome Estate in 1935 as being "On the Golders Green Tube Line", again in preference to the "new Met. station opening actually adjoining the estate". This preference for the "tubes" and their low fares was also demonstrated at Woodside Park in 1934, where F. J. C. Ingram offered his type 'A' house for £975 freehold or £815 leasehold with the attraction of hard tennis courts, cricket field and social club house. To get this new house and all these attractions, the fortunate purchaser was advised to go to Golders Green, thence by tram or bus, or to Wood Green or Highgate, thence tram or bus again. The option of approaching by LNER steam train to Woodside Park, itself only a short walk away, was a rather poor third!

Much of the development along the new extensions was built speculatively for purchase, but in Hendon, where land was expensive, many blocks of luxury flats were built and on both Edgware and Morden lines there was construction of council housing by the London County Council. The LCC had begun its policy of inner London slum clearance in the early years of the century, but the programme was given added impetus at the end of the First World War with a drive to build 'Homes for Heroes'. During construction of the Edgware line the LCC acquired 390 acres of land at Burnt Oak for one of its largest 'cottage estates' and by its completion in 1930 had built 4,021 houses and flats at weekly rents of 11/3 to 22/3 (56p to £1.11). Because of material shortages many of the houses were built of concrete or wood instead of brick, giving the estate a distinctive character to this day. As in the private sector, cheap and reliable transport was a prerequisite of successful development. In a similar – and huge – development at Becontree transport problems gave the council many headaches in filling the vacant properties. Some 9,000 dwellings were constructed in 1930-34 by the same builders for the LCC at St Helier, just south of Morden Station, with the attractive cottage style now modified with larger windows – and even bays – to resemble more closely the output for private purchasers.

Clearly the Northern was capable of attracting large accretions of housing to its new stations, but as the lines were built to full Underground standards they were relatively expensive to construct and operate. Efforts were therefore made to attract even more traffic through the operation of feeder bus services, tapping areas too distant to rely on walking. Thus Golders Green, Edgware and Morden were all provided with bus stations to facilitate easy and controlled interchange. Through fares were also offered at low rates and this, coupled with high frequencies, was enough to bring people in from a wide radius around the stations.

The need for these feeders was perhaps particularly significant at Edgware where there was some dissatisfaction with the rate of growth of the new suburb, and hence with the level of demand for the train service. The first new bus service started about three years after the opening of the railway. In the ensuing five years a substantial network was developed which effectively contributed to the factors mentioned earlier to suppress demand on the Stanmore Line, where ultimately each of the new stations was passed by buses running straight to Northern Line stations. The network thus created was to survive the creation of London Transport in 1933, and continue almost unchanged until the "Bus Reshaping Plan" started with its spread of one-person operation in the late 1960s.

Growth along the lines was sufficient to cause many complaints of rush hour overcrowding by the mid-1930s and the problem was debated everywhere from the local pub to the columns of the Times and in Parliament. Over the years various initiatives were tried to alleviate the difficulties and make services more attractive, including the operation of 'fast' trains non-stopping Brent (now Brent Cross) using bypass lines and later the running of some nine-car trains. Users also, of course, had to contend with the odd breakdown as well as chronic crowding. One Edgware resident had decided to use the line to get to her wedding at Hendon Synagogue in August 1936; imagine her consternation when she arrived at the station and found the trains had stopped running? Although the line did not have a reputation for particularly bad running the seeds of today's discontent had certainly been sown and cultivated by this time: in fact the first known 'sit in' strike by passengers refusing to detrain seems to have been as early as the mid-1930s.

Outside the busiest times the railway was used for more everyday leisure than in recent times. Evenings out tended to be held in the West End, whether at the theatre or to dine. 'London Town and Country', published by the Underground in 1928, urged residents to eat at the Frascati Restaurant after watching a show or, for those favouring something spicier, at Veerasawmy's Indian. At the weekends, the same book tempted Londoners to travel outwards, referring to the transformation at Edgware where "fields are giving way to houses, and the footpath of yesterday may be the suburban by-way of tomorrow". The suburbs had become an idyllic dream, offering contemporary families "country living" but with access to all London had to offer. The fact that the dream was self destructive, each new estate destroying a little more of the fields and woodlands which were so attractive, had eluded many. Similarly, to the Underground company there was an attraction in continually expanding and tapping new markets. This in itself was both understandable and commercially desirable, but as proposals for substantial new expansion were formulated by the new London Passenger Transport Board in 1933 it was apparent that the authorities had anticipated neither the political will to stop the greedy outward spread of houses nor the resistance of the daily user to travel long distances on tube trains designed for in-town traffic and stopping at stations at frequent intervals.

On 5th August 1935 an RAF plane from a flight leaving Hendon turned back with mechanical difficulties shortly after take-off. The plane lost height and crashed across the tracks, 200 yards away from Colindale station, killing the pilot. The short-circuit caused by the plane started a fire in Colindale signal cabin, which soon blazed out of control, totally destroying it. Courtesy of Lilian Bayman

As the 1930s – and peace – drew to a close, there was increasing concern about the ever outward spread of avenues and crescents in London. Various initiatives were under way to conserve undeveloped land but at best these could be considered piecemeal. The spirit of these ideas was embodied in a plan for Greater London, drawn up by Professor Abercrombie in 1944, which very much portrayed the 'Brave New World' looked forward to by war-weary Londoners by that time. In 1947 a new Town and Country Planning Act passed into law and provided a continuous Green Belt around London, effectively sealing its boundaries to the 1939 tidemark.

Housing development in the Greater London area was certainly not finished, though. The Green Belt had enclosed some pockets of unused land scheduled for housing, especially on estates under construction in 1939 which had not been completed before the war. Thus building continued to increase populations in outer London for some years, although it was not again to reach the scale of expansion of the 1930s. Sadly some of this infilling was on land previously owned by London Transport for the Northern extensions. Where infilling did take place it was invariably on a more intensive scale than before the war. This is readily discernible at Grahame Park, Colindale, where 1970s development on the former Hendon Aerodrome is much more densely packed than the estate constructed forty years earlier at Stag Lane Aerodrome, Burnt Oak.

Inevitably, major housing expansion was concentrated in a new ring outside the Green Belt. The first generation of new suburban dwellers was substantially still in occupation in the 1950s and 60s when their children needed homes of their own – this new generation left in droves to the affordable estates farther afield. This left the Underground with an ageing population and, in effect, with ageing industry to serve as well. It is thus not surprising that the once strong relationship between the Northern and its suburban communities weakened. Certainly through the early post-war decades the only sizeable growth in employment was among married women as families struggled to afford increasing commitments to consumer durables and holidays abroad: most of these worked locally and had no need for the Underground.

Changes in the suburban way of life were also affecting demand for leisure journeys. Even by 1950 those who would once have taken the tube to the country for a Sunday ramble were now starting to own motor cars and clog the roads to the coast. At the same time there were the first signs of the impending explosion in television ownership, which was to turn us from cinema and theatregoers into fireside families.

Before the War, air displays at RAF Hendon attracted huge crowds, most of whom chose to travel by the cheap and frequent tube services to Colindale. For many this was their first view of the new north London suburbs. LT Museum

The 1935-40 New Works Programme

1933 is well known as the year in which London Transport was created. It was on 1st July of that year that all the Underground railways, the buses and the trams were transferred to the new London Passenger Transport Board. Of course, many of the services had already been a part of the old Underground Group (including most of the buses and a proportion of the trams) but it was hoped that the enforced co-ordination would bring greater efficiency and better services.

Even more relevant was the simultaneous establishment of the London Passenger Transport Pool. This was administered by a Standing Joint Committee consisting of the new LPTB and representatives of the main line companies. Within the LPTB area all revenue related to local passenger journeys was pooled, and shared out in agreed proportions. This meant that developments and service alterations made by any one of the constituents would have an effect on the revenues of them all, though to different degrees. In turn it meant that there was an enforced measure of co-operation needed between members of the pool, and the Standing Joint Committee (rather than the LPTB alone) emerged as the central planning authority for London's new services.

Even in 1933 and 1934 considerable planning work was being done in the expectation that money would be made available for a substantial scheme of expansion. There were several areas around the system where there was a clear demand for service improvement or extension of services. On what was to become the Northern Line, the area north of Highgate frequently registered its dissatisfaction with existing transport facilities and previous extension had been contemplated (though never commanding priority). There was, for example, a proposal to extend the Highgate branch to Muswell Hill as long previously as 1919. It is worth the reminder that 'Highgate' is now the station we call Archway and that there was considerable latent capacity available after 1924, the Highgate branch having only three stations north of Camden Town against the nine of the Edgware branch.

Another line which came under the microscope was the former Great Northern & City Railway (opened in 1904) which sported only six stations and ran between Moorgate and Finsbury Park – unusually a tube railway built to main line gauge. Here, there was a large amount of awkward interchange at Finsbury Park from the main line and the buses and trams, yet the line itself had extra capacity available. Plans soon emerged for northward extension and through running upon the main line railway above.

What emerged after two years of rumours, debate and political manoeuvring was a massive scheme of improvements estimated to cost some £40 million. The money was to be raised by a statutory finance corporation at low interest and backed by a treasury guarantee. The work included replacement of trams by trolleybuses, some main line railway suburban electrification, Underground line modernisation, and projection of Underground trains over main line tracks, electrified for the purpose.

The effect on the Northern Line was a proposal to extend the Highgate branch northwards to East Finchley, thence take over the existing London & North Eastern Railway branches to High Barnet and Edgware. The existing station at Highgate would

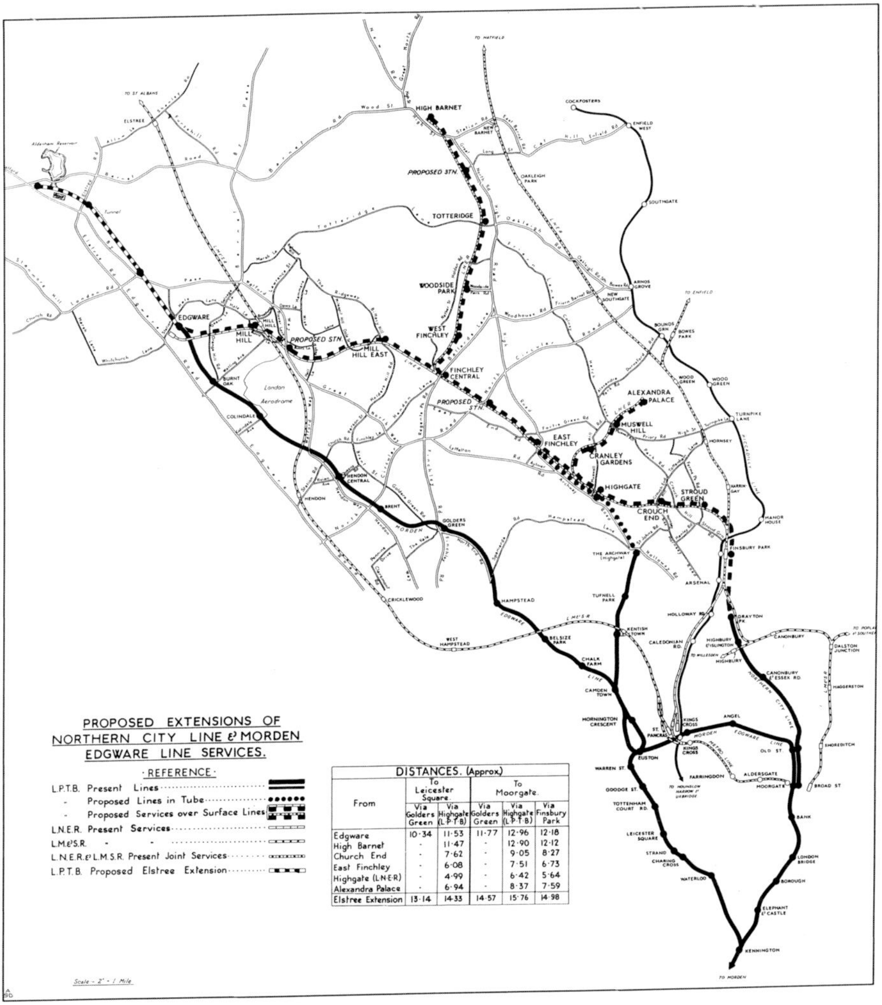

DISTANCES. (Approx.)					
From	To Leicester Square		To Moorgate.		
	Via Golders Green	Via Highgate (L·P·T·B)	Via Golders Green	Via Highgate (L·P·T·B)	Via Finsbury Park
Edgware	10·34	11·53	11·77	12·96	12·18
High Barnet	-	11·47	-	12·90	12·12
Church End	-	7·62	-	9·05	8·27
East Finchley	-	6·08	-	7·51	6·73
Highgate (L·N·E·R)	-	4·99	-	6·42	5·64
Alexandra Palace	-	6·94	-	8·37	7·59
Elstree Extension	13·14	14·33	14·57	15·76	14·98

be renamed Archway, and there would be an intermediate station beneath the existing Highgate (LNER) station, with which there would be interchange. An additional scheme emerged to link the Great Northern & City tube from Moorgate to a new line through Finsbury Park (LNER) station and thence take over the Alexandra Palace branch but with through trains also to the High Barnet and Edgware branches. The whole network would then be operated as one railway.

The LNER branch between Finsbury Park and Edgware had opened in 1867, with the Finchley – High Barnet section following in 1872 and Highgate – Alexandra Palace in 1873. By the early 1930s there were 54 trains a day from High Barnet and 43 from the Alexandra Palace branch. Edgware to Church End (at Finchley) was generally worked as a shuttle service, but with a few through trains. The service from these branches worked to King's Cross, Moorgate or Broad Street and the journey time from Barnet to Moorgate was around 47 minutes (present time for this journey is 38 minutes and there are over 130 trains to London destinations from Barnet alone).

The necessary powers were obtained in 1935 and 1936. Work on the link between Archway and East Finchley began in November 1936. This involved converting the northbound siding into the beginning of the new running tunnel while adapting the other siding into what would be a centre reversing siding. At the East Finchley end the new tube tunnels would emerge either side of the existing LNER line and then proceed into the station, which required complete rebuilding.

To make life even more interesting, it was realised that the existing depot accommodation would be inadequate for these much expanded services and consideration was given to an extension north of Edgware over the former Watford & Edgware Railway alignment to Aldenham, later referred to as Bushey Heath, where a large new depot would be erected. The area was almost entirely in open country and again there was a hope that speculative development would justify such an extension. The scheme required the complete rebuilding of Edgware Station to allow for through running either from the Golders Green direction or from Finchley, there being a link from the nearby LNER branch which was being electrified.

Work on the Edgware station reconstruction began in 1937 and eventually resulted in complete revision of the stabling siding layout and the demolition of the bus garage and the east wing of the station to allow for doubling the width of the station cutting. The station was to be rebuilt to allow large scale bus-rail interchange. The LNER line north of Finsbury Park was to be electrified and resignalled to Underground standards, most of which work was begun and continued while trains were running. Between Finchley Central and Edgware, however, the line was single track and would have to be doubled. To allow this work to proceed quickly the service between these two points was suspended from 10th September 1939 and a bus service substituted (this had operated previously during the midday period and on Sundays).

Bushey Heath station, at the junction of Elstree Road and the Watford By-Pass, was to be the focal point of a new shopping centre with a cinema and a pub opposite, and subways leading from the station underneath both roads. The station design bore a considerable resemblance to Cockfosters Piccadilly Line station.

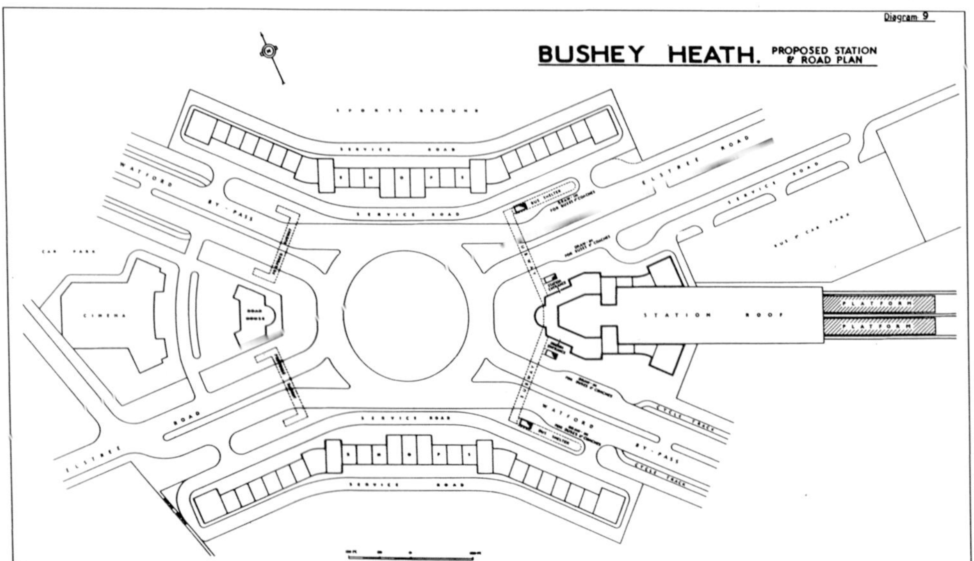

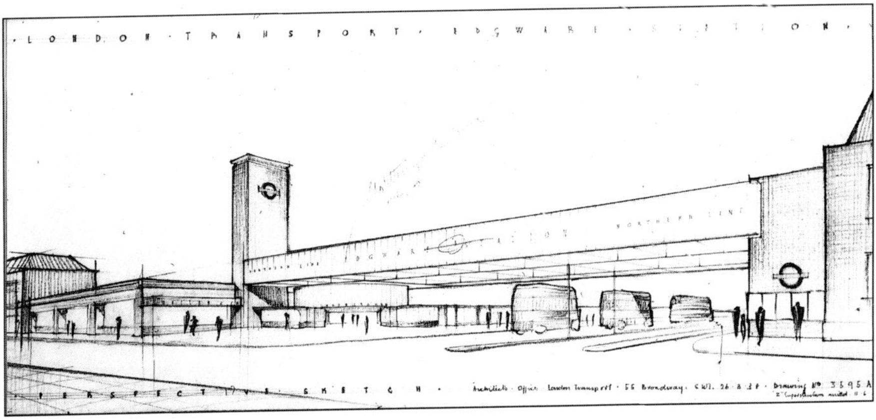

Access and interchange were planned for in all the new and modified stations. Edgware's successful bus feeder services were to be catered for by building a new covered bus station alongside, with an enlarged bus garage behind the station. A characteristic brick tower would emphasise the LPTB station presence with a highly visible roundel sign. At Mill Hill (The Hale) a new combined station building serving both LPTB and LM&SR stations would provide covered interchange, whilst a rebuilt forecourt proposed new shop units with improved foot and road access.

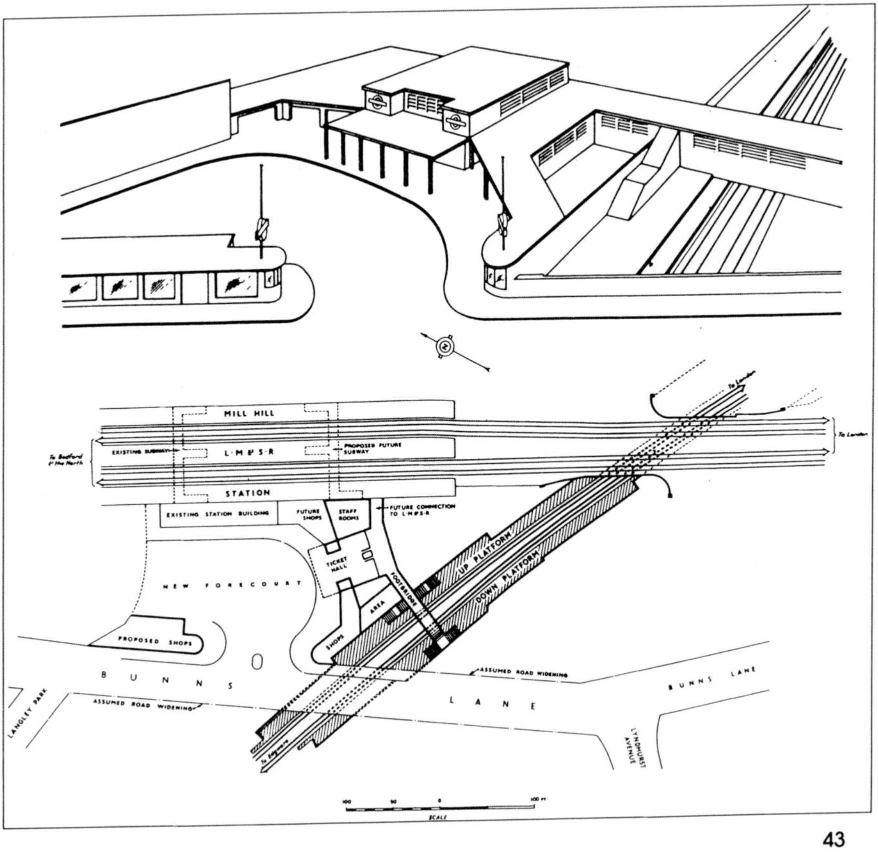

At Edgware reconstruction envisaged most of the trains from Bushey Heath running via Finchley Central, with services from both branches also terminating at Edgware. This post-war photo of Edgware shows the enlarged station and unused additional platforms. Photomatic

Facing Page **Arches constructed opposite the junction of Spur Road and the A41 at Edgware, the site of the planned Brockley Hill station. Bushey Heath Depot was to have become the main depot on the Northern Line, replacing the cramped facilities at Golders Green. The main depot buildings were constructed and equipped in advance of the trackwork, lest they be required for essential war work in the looming conflict, which they were. In this post-war view a hut has been added (left foreground) which partly obscures the workshop (extreme left).** Photomatic/LT Museum

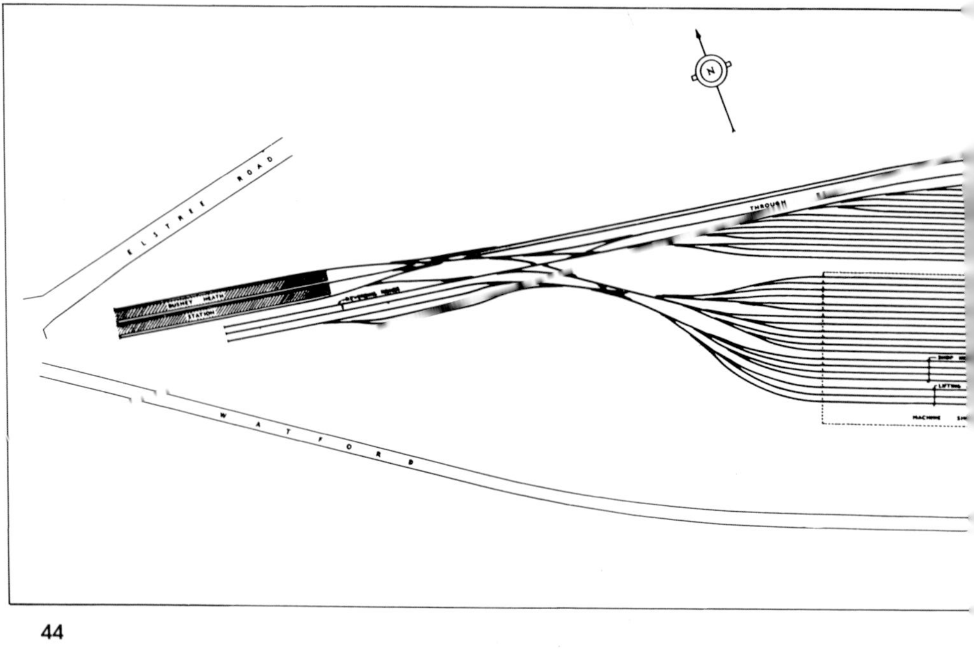

BUSHEY HEATH DEPOT - PROPOSED LAYOUT

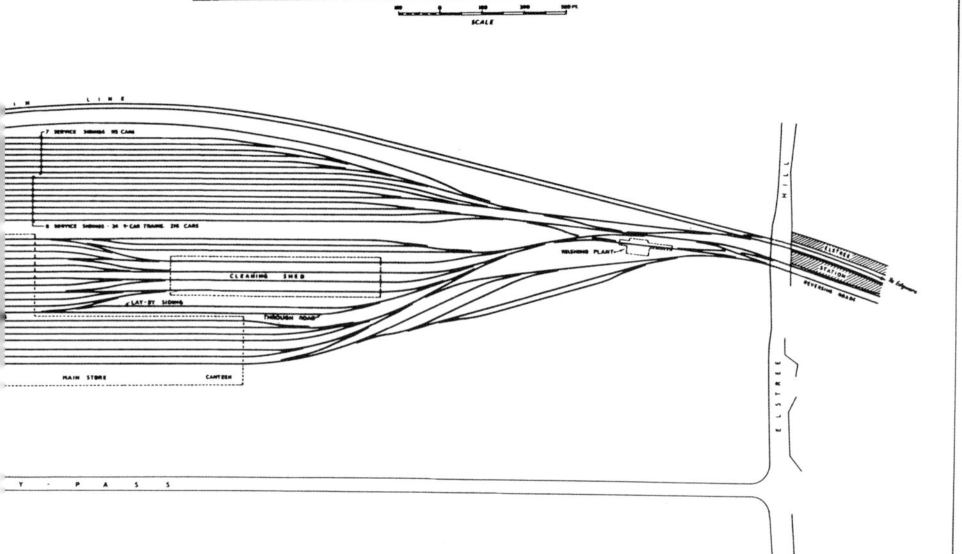

With the extension of the Northern Line to East Finchley, the original GNR station building dating from the 1860s was demolished and a new building to the design of Adams, Holden and Pearson was constructed. By the northern bridge abutment a 10ft-high statue of an archer was erected, now the house symbol of the Northern Line. LT Museum

Early plans considered the possibility of building additional stations between Totteridge and High Barnet, between East Finchley and Church End (which became Finchley Central) and between Mill Hill East and Mill Hill (The Hale). None of these were pursued at the time and subsequent events failed to indicate any current need. Elsewhere it was intended to provide entirely reconstructed stations at East Finchley, Finchley Central (which would gain a fourth platform), Mill Hill (The Hale), Edgware and High Barnet. The East Finchley station was completed almost in entirety and sported a large sculpture in the form of an Archer. Only minor work was undertaken at Finchley Central – including part of the new platform – and for reasons to be given shortly little other work was done, existing stations having to suffice.

At Drayton Park work began on constructing ramps up to surface level and the whole of the Great Northern & City Railway was modernised with the standard current rail system and modern signalling. This required replacing the existing type of sub-surface rolling stock with standard tube stock. The extension between Archway and East Finchley opened on 3rd July 1939, although the intermediate Highgate station was not ready until April 1941.

Scenes at East Finchley two weeks before the Northern Line arrived. LNER steam passes the newly built signal box, while a large banner straddles the Great North Road to announce the impending introduction of Underground services. J. Bonell

Edgware station, LNER, which closed to passengers in April 1940. A Sainsbury's supermarket occupies most of this land today.

Highgate's New Station

The combined station at Highgate had four entrances: the entrance from the Archway Road by the 'Woodman' public house was to have a pair of escalators to traverse the sixty or so feet from pavement to platform. In the event this part of the scheme was deferred and it was not until August 1957 that a single up escalator was put into service. M.A.C. Horne

UNDERGROUND UNDER L·N·E·R

ESCALATOR TO ALEXANDRA PALACE LINE

An Addition to the Northern Line

To operate the Northern Line extensions additional rolling stock was necessary. It was eventually decided to provide the Northern Line entirely with new high-capacity trains, and to transfer the existing trains to other lines. The new stock was smart and had semi-streamlined cabs; the main development introduced on these trains was compressors and motor control equipment being mounted underfloor which, together with more compact motors, allowed the whole of the car interiors to be utilised for passenger accommodation. The practical effect of this was that a 7-car train of the new type had the same carrying capacity as an 8-car train of the old. The new trains became known as the 1938 stock, and the Northern Line was completely re-equipped between June 1938 and 1940.

Nine-car trains were one of a number of ideas tried in an attempt to increase the capacity of the Northern Line. Following experimental work, a single 9-car train was introduced from November 1937. From February 1938 several trains were operated on the West End branch and they became a regular feature. Platform lengths between Golders Green and Edgware were increased by an appropriate amount, but only minor changes were made at tunnel stations. The restricted tunnel platforms meant that two cars would be beyond the platform and the mode of operation was that advance warning was given to passengers that the rear two cars would stop in the tunnel between Hampstead and Kennington southbound, except at Tottenham Court Road where these cars would then empty. Northbound, the front cars were cut out between Kennington and Leicester Square, the rear cars being cut out between Tottenham Court Road and Golders Green. For the guard to be able to keep a look out at all stations he had to ride on the seventh car, and was provided with various door cut-out switches to ensure that only doors in the platform opened. There were thoughts of substantial numbers of 9-car trains being introduced to service the new extensions, and extensive provision for them was proposed in terms of platform and siding lengths. In the event only ten 1938 stock trains were planned as 9-car trains, and wartime conditions put paid to this idiosyncratic mode of operation with only the first two having entered service.

The 1938 Stock benefited from developments in mechanical design which allowed much control equipment to be located beneath seats and under the floor. Consequently the interior was uncluttered and provided more seats and far greater standing area than the cars which it replaced. LT Museum

The Northern Line at War

War came a little early to the Northern Line. Air raids had become a feature of the latter part of the First World War, and Blitzkrieg tactics had been well demonstrated during the Spanish Civil War. Two years later, in the autumn of 1938, came the threat of German expansion: when this culminated in the Munich Crisis talks, Britain was alive to the threat of imminent bombing. It was recognised that London would be in the forefront of the attacks; also that the Underground network was under threat from flooding through bombed water mains or penetration of the cross-Thames tubes.

Given this threat, and fearing the flooding of the entire central London network, it was understandable that drastic measures should be taken, although it must have been of some surprise to south London theatregoers on the evening of 27th September 1938 to find that the tube which had taken them to the West End was no longer available to take them home. During the evening, services had been withdrawn between Strand (now Charing Cross) and Kennington, and over the following hours the tunnels were plugged with concrete to seal them against flooding. This particular disruption, though serious, was fairly short-lived. Neville Chamberlain had soon returned with a promise of 'Peace in our time', and the crisis was over. The concrete was broken out and the West End branch lived again on 8th October. It had been, of course, a grim foretaste of what was to follow.

The late 1930s had been promising for the Northern Line – it was facing expansion, to the North at least, into new areas where the fields of the Elstree Heights would soon become leafy new suburbs. The clerks and businessmen would be carried back from City offices to their families in modern streamlined trains – trains which would in turn benefit from the new depot facilities near Aldenham, a far cry from the Edwardian sheds at Golders Green. At weekends, ramblers would be carried in droves to the hills beyond Edgware to picnic in the meadows.

The first part of the promise was fulfilled on 3rd July 1939, when services were extended from Archway to the bold new station at East Finchley, to connect with the steam services to High Barnet and Edgware. As families first used this route out of London for days in the country it became clear that something was wrong: an era was coming to a close. Only weeks later, on 1st September, carefully prepared plans to evacuate children got under way. To reduce congestion at main line termini, plans included the use of the Underground to carry children to outer suburban railheads, where fleets of buses carried them to the main line. Thus train-loads of youngsters – some eager to start a new life, but others in tears – were carried out to Edgware and thence by bus to New Barnet and the north. On the same day the link between Strand and Kennington was again lost, the tunnels plugged once more and work started on installing floodgates so that services could continue away from the Thames during raids (it would otherwise have been necessary to close the entire central area network). War was, of course, declared on 3rd September with an immediate reduction in optional traffic: people stayed at home; for a few weeks at least all theatres and cinemas closed. Art galleries and some offices had also left London for the duration.

NOTICE

NORTHERN LINE

From September 7th, the section of the Northern Line between London Bridge and Moorgate will be closed

The section between Kennington and Strand will remain closed

Extra buses will be placed on bus routes serving

MOORGATE
BANK
LONDON BRIDGE

Railway tickets will be available on the bus services between London Bridge and Moorgate

Until further notice the Northern Line trains will then only operate between

Morden, Kennington and London Bridge
Moorgate and E. Finchley & Edgware
Strand and East Finchley & Edgware

CLOSING OF STATIONS

ON AND FROM SEPTEMBER 7

In order that certain work may be carried out, it has become necessary to close until further notice, the following stations entirely, except that the interchange subways will be available at the stations marked thus*

Arsenal
Balham
†Bank {NORTHERN LINE / CENTRAL LINE}
Bond Street
Chancery Lane
Charing Cross {BAKERLOO LINE / NORTHERN LINE}
Clapham Common
Green Park
Hyde Park Corner
Kings Cross {PICCADILLY LINE / NORTHERN LINE}
Knightsbridge
Maida Vale
Marble Arch
Old Street
Oval
*Oxford Circus
*Tottenham Ct. Rd.
Trinity Road
Waterloo NORTHERN LINE

† The ticket hall and lifts at Bank (Northern Line) station will remain open to provide access to Central Line trains and to the subway connection with Monument.

AVAILABILITY OF TICKETS. Holders of current season tickets available at stations closed may, if they wish, surrender their tickets at any Ticket Office (or by post to the Commercial Manager, London Transport, 55 Broadway, S.W.1), and they will in due course receive a full refund for the unused period as from the date of surrender. Owing to the exceptional circumstances, it will not be possible to ensure that accommodation for season ticket holders will be available on alternative road or rail services, but such passengers may use them if they can. Single and return journey tickets will not be available on alternative road or rail services. CLOAK ROOM deposits will be removed from the closed stations to the Lost Property Office at 200, Baker Street (adjoining Baker Street station), where they may be claimed on Mondays to Fridays only between 10 a.m. and 7 p.m.

In addition, the train service on the Northern Line will not run between Kennington and Strand or between London Bridge and Moorgate. The availability of tickets will be as above, except that between Kennington and Strand single and return journey tickets will be available by alternative rail services; between London Bridge and Moorgate such tickets will be available by alternative road services.

Posters announcing the closure of stations near the Thames or close to water mains so that tunnels or escalator shafts in danger of flooding by bomb damage could be plugged.

Although the cross-Thames tunnels on the City Branch were significantly deeper than those to the west, it was quickly realised that these also presented a risk of breach and on 7th September they too were plugged. Services from the north thus terminated at Moorgate and Strand, while trains from Morden terminated no further north than London Bridge: the Northern was cut in two. This caused extensive congestion on parallel bus and tram routes.

It was also necessary to close a number of stations which were regarded as ‘low lying’ and in danger of flooding the system in the event of water mains being hit. Seven of these were on the Northern: Tooting Broadway, Tooting Bec (then Trinity Road), Balham, Clapham Common, Old Street, King’s Cross and Tottenham Court Road. In all cases street access was blocked by concrete plugs but interchange between lines was still possible at the last three (a situation which would not be allowed by today’s safety considerations).

The blackout was also a problem – gallons of white paint were used on obstructions at open stations as a substitute for lighting but this did nothing to help identification of the hapless passenger’s destination. Windows were by this time covered with anti-blast netting which rendered identification of surroundings quite impossible after dark. The driver’s lookout window did not, of course, have netting but even so station staff had to provide a hurricane lamp by the stopping mark at each platform to assist drivers. The drivers themselves were also under instruction to coast as much as possible – to save energy – but also particularly over current rail gaps to minimise the risk of arcing which is highly visible from the air after dark.

Blast shelters were erected outside all stations — as here at Goodge Street — to minimise the effect of a bomb exploding nearby. Like all pavement obstructions the blast shelters were prominently edged with white paint to be distinguishable in black-out conditions. LT Museum

During air raids, those sections of the Underground running under the Thames were closed and, at first, the use of Underground stations as shelters was forbidden.

AIR RAIDS

During an air raid or when an ALERT is sounded, trains will cease to run on the following sections of the Underground

NORTHERN LINE	Bank to London Bridge Strand to Kennington via Charing Cross and Waterloo
BAKERLOO LINE	Piccadilly Circus to Elephant & Castle via Charing Cross and Waterloo Special buses will run between Piccadilly Circus and Elephant & Castle via Charing Cross Underground Station
EAST LONDON LINE	Shoreditch to Surrey Docks

AVAILABILITY OF TICKETS

Passengers already holding tickets available at closed stations may travel to or from any other London Transport station in the vicinity and by any alternative Underground route. If no such route is available passengers may make or complete their journeys by bus tram or trolleybus without extra payment. At closed stations the ticket office will remain open for the sale of rail tickets which passengers can then use for travel by the alternative routes

WAR EMERGENCY

UNDERGROUND STATIONS MUST NOT BE USED AS AIR RAID SHELTERS

The public are informed that in order to operate the Railways for essential movement, Underground Stations cannot be used as air raid shelters. In any event a number of stations would have to be cleared for safety in certain contingencies

UNDERGROUND

Apart from making life difficult for regular operations, the blackout also made engineering work take much longer than before: it is recorded that a derailment at East Finchley early in 1940 took many hours to rectify and caused extreme disruption. Work on the unfinished extensions also slowed down, and ironically steam passenger services were withdrawn between Finchley Central and Edgware on 10th September 1939 "to facilitate works". Bus services were provided as a substitute and it was to be that passenger services were never restored between Mill Hill East and Edgware.

The early months of the war had proved to be something of an anti-climax. There was a little time to provide refinements here and there: for example, passengers on trains were provided with dim blue lighting and reading lights for use in the open sections, although the latter were extinguished during raids. Everyone was asked to 'dig for victory' – many trackside stretches were converted to allotments by staff and neighbours, and proved quite long lasting; some in the vicinity of Whetstone and High Barnet were still going strong until considerations for safety and the 'weed-killing' train finally extinguished them in the mid-1980s. Land in Underground ownership for the extensions was cultivated for canteen produce and the horses used there were fed on hay from embankments around the system.

Although the Underground was officially a 'protected industry', avoiding major loss of labour to the armed forces, many employees did enter the King's service. It was necessary, as in the First World War, to bring women into uniformed jobs then regarded as the property of men. The first started work in September 1940: after the war numbers of women declined and it was not until the late 1970s that any significant headway was made by women into the industry again.

The quieter period in the early months had seen the progressive provision of floodgates in stations and tunnels, allowing through services to be resumed on the Charing Cross branch on 17th December 1939, and through the city on 19th May 1940. The new gates restricted platform lengths, however, and special instructions were issued to guards concerning door operation at Waterloo and London Bridge.

Work on the extensions had allowed the Northern to replace steam passenger services to High Barnet on 14th April 1940, giving the Northern the distinction of being the only line extended during the war. From this date the London Transport fare-scale applied, although the line remained in main line ownership. At the same time the ticket office at the LNER station at Edgware was closed to passengers and its business was transferred to the Underground station a few hundred yards away – in practice this simply involved moving the ticket stock and the turning point for the railway replacement bus service.

The new Highgate station was opened in an incomplete state in January 1941 – it was over a decade before further works were carried out – and there was a final extension from Finchley Central to Mill Hill East on 18th May 1941 to serve the Inglis Barracks (the bus shuttle was cut back to run between Edgware and Mill Hill East at the same time). The remaining extension works had been abandoned in June 1940 "for the duration", although new trains continued to arrive until 1941, displacing other stock for storage and ultimate use on the Central Line.

The electrification of the Alexandra Palace branch came to grief, despite the considerable work completed, although this branch did enter the London Transport fares system. Initially the steam train services from Finsbury Park continued to operate both to Alexandra Palace and to East Finchley (offering cross-platform interchange with electric services northwards). The East Finchley steam service was withdrawn from 3rd March 1941 (requiring rather less convenient interchange at Highgate), while the Alexandra Palace steam service gradually degenerated.

Serious loss of life and major disruption was caused by a bomb which exploded underground at Balham station on 14th October 1940. LT Museum

Work on the section north of Edgware had only begun fairly late in 1939 and took the form of earthworks, construction of twin-tube tunnels and depot buildings at Aldenham. When this work, too, stopped late in 1940 there was little to show, though the partly built tunnels were appreciated by the military who adapted them as a firing range. The depot buildings were pushed forward in an adapted form and became part of an aircraft factory as part of a scheme run by London Transport to construct Halifax bombers.

The opportunity was also taken in this period to develop staff procedures. Early in 1940 staff were instructed on the handling of the various categories of raid alert (not all of which were declared publicly) and provision was made for the control function to move during raids from Leicester Square to underground locations at Camden Town and Kennington for the northern and southern sections of the line respectively. As thoughts returned to the more dire considerations of invasion it was recognised that the Underground offered excellent opportunities for enemy troop movements, which were to be prevented by the simple expedient of discharging traction current.

During the raids in 1917 residents had taken to the Underground to shelter. This time round the government feared that a 'deep shelter mentality' would develop, with people refusing to come out. At the outset of the war the use of Underground stations as shelters was therefore banned. This caused few problems during the 'phoney war' period but once the enemy's attention was turned towards Britain in 1940 circumstances changed dramatically. Air raids started in August of that year: by the following month, whatever the wishes of the authorities, Underground stations were de facto deep level shelters.

The steel-framed construction of Camden Town station saved it from greater damage when it was hit in autumn 1940. LT Museum

The government soon acknowledged reality and recognised that the demand for a quiet night amongst the inner-city dwellers could not be ignored (it was also realised that fears of people refusing to leave after raids were actually ill-founded). It was also later noticeable that the platforms were becoming rather smelly, and by October provisions were in hand for improved sanitation and for bunks. Demand was high; tickets were issued and it was decided to open both the disused stations at South Kentish Town and City Road, and the unfinished station at Highgate. Special trains were run to convey shelterers to and from these locations and later on specials were run to carry refreshments too. The shelterers came to be quite at home on the tube over the twelve months from August 1940: some were even born there. The presence of these refugees from the noise of bombs and anti-aircraft fire did not help the passage of those still on their way home to the more distant suburbs though – thousands of passengers had to pick their way over slumbering bodies and sometimes by mid-evening stations were closed to avoid danger from congestion. Borough station, for example, was closed at 9 o'clock in the evening on 12th September 1940 owing to enormous congestion of people taking shelter from air raids. The disused C&SLR tunnels from Borough to King William Street were also converted for use as air raid shelters.

LONDON TRANSPORT in conjunction with The LOCAL AUTHORITY

Admit one Person for Shelter (if available) at

KENNINGTON Station

Subject to the Conditions shown on back

AVAILABLE NIGHT OF ISSUE ONLY

NOT TRANSFERABLE or AVAILABLE FOR TRAVEL

Persons who enter or remain on the premises of the Board for the purpose of AIR RAID SHELTER do so at their own risk in all respects, and neither the Board nor their Servants or Agents shall be responsible to such persons or their dependants for personal injury (whether fatal or otherwise) loss of or damage to property or any other loss, damage costs or expenses however caused or incurred.

National Registration No.

LONDON CIVIL DEFENCE REGION **No.** ....

METROPOLITAN BOROUGH OF ST. PANCRAS

Admit person named below for shelter at

MORNINGTON CRESCENT STATION

Name .... Age ....

Address ....

Nature of Employment ....

Date of Issue ....

C. S. BAINBRIDGE,
A.R.P. Controller

Signature of Issuing Officer.

PERSONS PERMITTED TO USE THIS STATION AS, OR AS A MEANS OF ACCESS TO, AN AIR RAID SHELTER, DO SO AT THEIR OWN RISK IN ALL RESPECTS.

NOT TRANSFERABLE. FOR FURTHER CONDITIONS OF ISSUE SEE BACK.

This ticket expires on **March 31st, 1942**

CONDITIONS OF ISSUE

1. This Ticket is issued subject to the London Regional Commissioners' Shelter Rules, copies of which are exhibited at the stations.
2. This Ticket does not permit the holder to travel on any portion of the London Passenger Transport Board's system. Where, however, the entrance to the station where the holder is entitled to shelter is closed, he will be entitled to travel free between the nearest open station and his shelter station.
3. Neither the Board nor their servants or agents shall be responsible to the holder or his dependants for personal injury (whether fatal or otherwise), loss of or damage to property, or any other loss, damage, costs or expenses, however caused or incurred.
4. This Ticket may be withdrawn or cease to be valid without any reason being given and, in particular, in ANY of the following circumstances :—
   a. If the station ceases to be available.
   b. If the holder of this Ticket, or any member of his family, commits any offence or creates any nuisance or disturbance in the station, or fails to do his share in keeping that portion of the station occupied by him tidy and clean.
   c. If the holder, being responsible for children fails to keep them under control and in particular allows them to play on escalators, lifts or trains.
   d. If the reserved space on the station premises is not used by the holder for four consecutive nights without explanation.
   e. If the holder disregards any lawful order or request of a Police Officer, Warden, Board's Official or any other authorised officer.
5. No person suffering from an infectious disease or coming from a house where there is an infectious disease will be allowed to use a Tube station as a shelter.
6. No bedding or belongings to be brought into the station before the appointed time and all bedding or belongings must be removed each morning.
7. No person will be allowed to use a Tube station as a shelter if his person, clothing or bedding is offensively unclean or is verminous.
8. No animals may be taken into the station.

USE YOUR STATION QUIETLY AND REGULARLY. HELP TO KEEP IT TIDY AND CLEAN.

The number on this Ticket corresponds with the space in the station reserved for the holder. The Ticket must not be used for any other accommodation.

The start of the blitz in August 1940 brought problems peculiar to the Northern, in that with each raid the cross-Thames sections were closed down, dividing the line into two. The low-lying stations were also closed and made watertight. This action certainly saved the day at Tooting Broadway on 7th October 1940, when a 30-inch (760mm) water main was destroyed just outside the station. On the other hand, with a relatively low proportion of its route in the open air, the Northern managed to escape some of the lengthy disruption experienced elsewhere on the surface.

There were, regrettably, two major incidents affecting the line – one at Bank in January 1941 when the subway system serving the Central Line ticket hall suffered a direct hit; the other, more seriously for the Northern, when a bomb breached the tunnels at Balham station, filling the platforms and tunnels to within 100 yards of Clapham South with soil, water and gas from shattered mains.

In some ways more disruptive, though, were the persistent closures and instances of damage from more minor incidents which affected service, staff and passengers on a daily basis for a year. Unexploded bombs sometimes caused service suspensions – two weeks in one case, between Golders Green and Colindale because of the threat from a bomb at

Facing Page **Two types of tickets were eventually issued for those seeking shelter in tube stations. The standard reservation ticket was issued by local authorities and bore a number which corresponded to a platform position — either bunk or floor space. The smaller blue card ticket was issued to casual shelterers, for whom an average of 10% of the accommodation was kept free.** M.A.C. Horne Collection

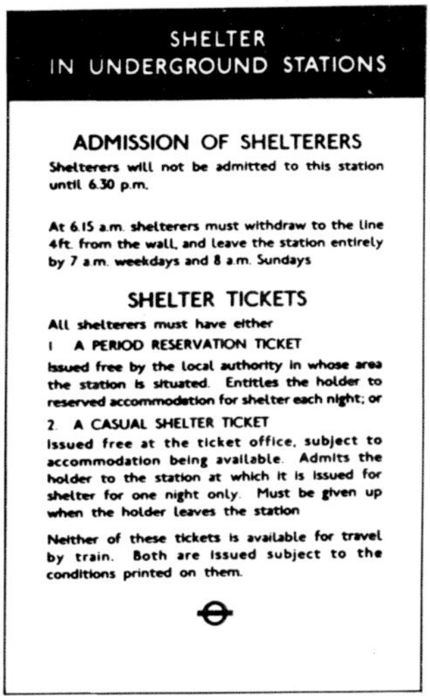

SHELTER
IN UNDERGROUND STATIONS

ADMISSION OF SHELTERERS

Shelterers will not be admitted to this station until 6.30 p.m.

At 6.15 a.m. shelterers must withdraw to the line 4ft. from the wall, and leave the station entirely by 7 a.m. weekdays and 8 a.m. Sundays

SHELTER TICKETS

All shelterers must have either

1 A PERIOD RESERVATION TICKET

Issued free by the local authority in whose area the station is situated. Entitles the holder to reserved accommodation for shelter each night; or

2. A CASUAL SHELTER TICKET

Issued free at the ticket office, subject to accommodation being available. Admits the holder to the station at which it is issued for shelter for one night only. Must be given up when the holder leaves the station

Neither of these tickets is available for travel by train. Both are issued subject to the conditions printed on them.

Special shelter arrangements were made by many authorities for those children not evacuated from London. On the platform wall can be seen the bunk position numbers, duplicated on shelter tickets. The posters give general guidance and instructions to adult shelterers. LT Museum

RAF Hendon. The booking hall at Colindale station was itself destroyed by enemy action in September 1940. On this occasion, a number of passengers on a train which had just arrived at the station were cut by flying glass. For over two hours the crew, aided by others, helped passengers to safety from the train and from the collapsed station buildings and staircase. The same station was hit again only a few days later, when staff had to escort passengers from a damaged train by a tortuous route to the street.

Staff were often kept busy dealing with the effects of minor damage – an example is Elephant & Castle, which received an incendiary hit on 7th September 1940. The canopy caught fire but, with the assistance of train staff, the fire was under control within ten minutes and the station saved, although passengers were diverted by way of the Bakerloo station until the integrity of the structure was confirmed. The tunnels themselves, although offering significant security, were not totally safe. The guard of a train at Borough two days after the incident at Elephant reported to the Station Master that he heard "loud reports which shook the tunnel". Following trains ran at reduced speed until inspections confirmed that all was well. The intensity of the raid also caused the Supervisor at Oval to close his station for fear of the welfare of passengers. Disruption on the day in question had been widespread; the service had already been reduced by the cancellation of many trains into service from Highgate following the discovery of an unexploded bomb at Wellington sidings at 6 o'clock in the morning.

This pattern, so early in the blitz, was to be repeated daily for twelve months. Apart from damage from incendiary and high explosive bombs, stations frequently had to close because of dangerous structures nearby or because of flooding – through fire hoses or damaged mains. Cables were also vulnerable to damage, often delaying traffic by disrupting signalling. Everybody was on edge: vigilant neighbours to the line just south of High Barnet reported a hole in the embankment at Sherrards Way, causing much alarm, but it was found to be nothing more sinister than the results of a local dog rooting around for its bone.

And so the story went on, with all sections of the Northern and Northern City Lines suffering damage from time to time and, during the year, virtually all stations on the line suffering some damage – with particular concentrations at London Bridge and at the stations in inner south London.

During the early days of the blitz it was decided to build new deep level shelters on the Northern alignment, with a view to these ultimately forming the route of an express post-war line from Golders Green (and possibly Finchley) in the north, by way of Waterloo and Clapham to areas unserved by the Underground in the Southern Railway's territory – Motspur Park and Chessington were in the planners' minds. These grandiose schemes did not, of course, reach fruition, but the shelters were built at Belsize Park, Camden Town, Goodge Street, Stockwell, Clapham North, Clapham Common and Clapham South. They were finished by September 1942 and were used initially for military purposes, the enemy's attention having turned away from England for the time being. When the 'V' bomb raids started in 1944 some of them were opened to the public for their originally intended purpose. The shelters still exist and are largely rented out for secure storage.

By the time the war was over, staff and passengers alike were weary but jubilant. Trains and other equipment had been run into the ground, maintenance facilities having been put to excellent use to overhaul tanks and manufacture aircraft. Much of the City had been razed and travel patterns had altered enormously. As the crowds celebrated peace in 1945 everybody looked forward to starting again where they had left off in 1939. Events were to prove them wrong.

Colindale station, lying close to RAF Hendon and local factories, was particularly vulnerable to enemy action. The original 1924 station building was completely destroyed by a direct bomb hit in September 1940. A temporary wooden ticket hall was constructed which lasted for over twenty years until a new ticket hall was built as part of a large office development.
LT Museum

The Northern Since the War

As we have seen, the once ambitious extensions to the north fell from favour during the early 1950s despite early assurances that all works would be resumed, and were abandoned progressively to 1954 when the wholly inadequate steam services to Alexandra Palace were withdrawn. Main line freight services continued to Alexandra Palace until 1958, to High Barnet until 1962, and to Edgware (via Mill Hill) until 1964. From the late 1950s much of the track bed was sold and building work was underway between Highgate, Muswell Hill and Alexandra Palace and north of Edgware. Soon afterwards the alignment was destroyed south of Mill Hill (The Hale) by housing and, later, the M1 motorway. The track between Highgate depot and Finsbury Park was retained for a few years more for (ironically enough) the use of occasional London Transport trains making their way under battery-hauled power to and from the isolated Northern City branch. These trains were, of course, devoid of passengers. The pre-war schemes had withered and died.

Curiously, the ticket system carried on for a while as though the electrification had proceeded. Tickets continued to be available for travel to Mill Hill (The Hale) and Edgware on the local bus (which had taken over this role from the special service) until as recently as the late 1960s, and it was even possible to issue season tickets on this route, though only to a diminishing number of regular holders.

Although scheduled steam services from High Barnet ceased when Northern Line services were extended there on 14th April 1940, excursions operated until summer 1956. The last steam train to High Barnet was in 1961 and the diesel-hauled freight trains continued until the goods yard was closed in October 1962. Derrick Bridges

Below **Initially after the war it had been intended that work on the Northern Line extensions would continue. This car map dates from 1948.**

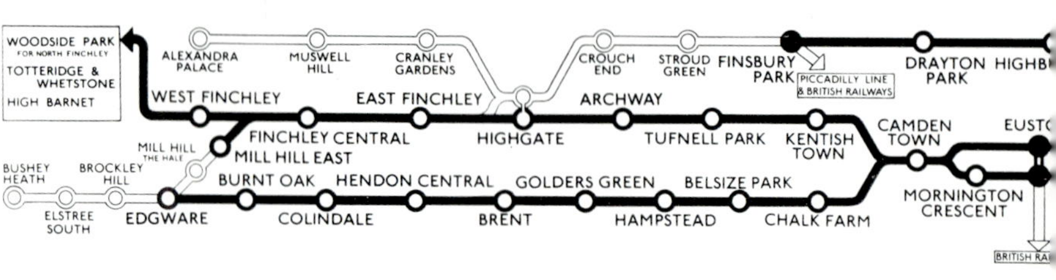

Scheduled steam services from East Finchley to King's Cross, Moorgate, Finsbury Park and Broad Street ceased in March 1941 following the opening of Highgate Northern Line platform. Occasional steam railtours, however, continued to visit the line until 1961. Fred Ivey

The Alexandra Palace service had operated only in peak hours from 1942, with through services beyond Finsbury Park being withdrawn. This diverted most potential traffic to parallel bus services. With the abandonment of the electrification proposals, British Railways, who were responsible for operating the line, successfully proposed closure. The last train ran on 3rd July 1954. Don Jones

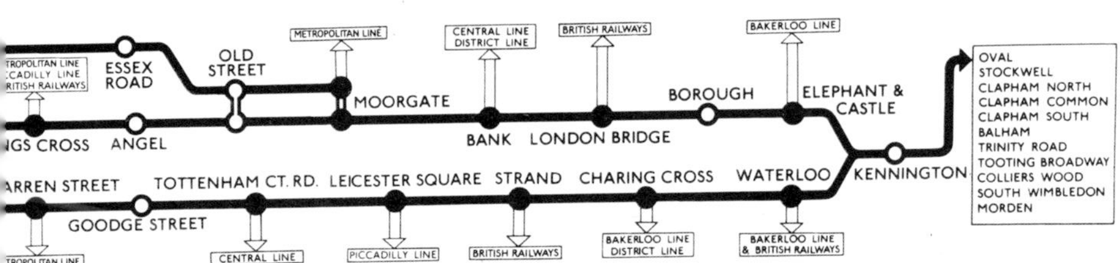

The early post-war years represented a high point for the Northern which was to remain unchallenged for over thirty years. Passenger demand peaked in 1948 but then entered a decline, unbroken for 34 years. Similarly, services reached a post-war peak at much the same time with an intensity and quality which is likely to remain unmatched until nearly the turn of the century, although even in 1948 frequencies had failed to match those of the 1930s.

With hindsight, it is perhaps now easy to see where and why things began to go wrong for the line. For a start, the pre-war regime of a transport board and traffic pool were superseded in 1948 by nationalisation of the vast majority of the inland transport system which became controlled by the British Transport Commission. The former LPTB lines (and parts of the main line now run by LPTB trains) were delegated to a London Transport Executive which had to vie with the capital-hungry Railway Executive for scarce funds (it was not until 1963 that London Transport gained fully independent status as a nationalised industry).

There was an understandable drive for cost efficiency throughout the Underground, given added momentum by the declining traffic. This was to lead to several economies, not least in the abandonment of traditional signal cabins which were replaced during the latter part of the period with a consequent loss of refinement of control and of communication between control staff and train drivers. The centralisation of signalling control on the Northern had started in the 1950s using programme machines, working on the principle of a 'pianola roll' providing routine schedule information, leaving the signalman to make adjustments from the central control only when necessary.

The Northern had been wholly converted to this form of operation by the early 1970s, but already the shortcomings of the system were clearly visible. No longer was the signalman an integral part of the service – now he sat very much on the outside and lacked the early warning 'feel' of trouble. Corrective action was slow to follow and when disruption came it was impossible for each signalman (now 'regulator') to cope with manual control in his vastly increased area. Without any means of positively identifying each train it was very easy to lose knowledge of which train was which – a problem anywhere but disastrous on a line as complex as the Northern. To add to this problem, the programme machines could count the passage of time only in chunks of half-minutes which is not helpful for junctions which are, say, 12 seconds from the timing point.

In 1958, to improve passenger journey time, two original lifts at Hampstead were replaced by the latest high speed lifts. At stations where traffic levels had not already justified conversion from lift to escalator access, there was also a need by the 1960s to replace the original lift equipment. With almost every lift unique in its length of travel, its equipment space and its ease of access, replacement has been lengthy and expensive.
LT Museum

Until the 1950s there was a seemingly unending queue of high calibre people waiting to work for London Transport. This scenario was to change abruptly through the decade with the well-known consequence of the organisation looking overseas to supplement domestic recruitment. This policy was, understandably, not without its problems and was only partially successful, so that by the mid-1960s services were suffering through labour shortage. This was unfortunate, for in 1967 training started of staff for the Victoria Line. The Victoria was one-person operated from the outset; the train operator becoming the most highly paid of train staff and thereby creaming the most senior and experienced drivers from around the system. As the Northern, with its old trains, lengthy tunnel running and middle-class depot locations, found recruitment difficult it suffered a particular concentration of trouble and services became less reliable. The press made direct comparisons between the sparkling new line and the tarnished Northern, especially at Highbury where the comparison between the new finishes of the Victoria and the unlined tunnel iron on the Northern City, literally a couple of paces away, was particularly stark.

Worse was to come. In 1969, before the services or the image of the Northern Line had any time to recover, a dispute at the Underground's central overhaul works at Acton cut off the supply of overhauled components, which particularly affected the compressors on 1938 stock trains running on the Northern and Bakerloo Lines. Within weeks up to a third of the Northern service was cancelled and a number of the trains still running had only six cars instead of seven. The level of service was clearly appalling, but the public relations people of the day tried to play the matter down and hardly acknowledged the problems, even to commuters with decades of experience. The result of this policy was that the community lost confidence and faith. Action groups were formed – some very powerful and vociferous. Late in the dispute the management became more honest, but it was too late. The damage was done; the line became known as 'the Misery Line' and its image destroyed even to this day.

Recovery was slow – by 1974 staff were being lost from the Underground in numbers far more than recruitment could cope with and, for the reasons mentioned above, the Northern was amongst the lines most seriously affected. The position did then improve through some heavy pay awards, but by this time the trains themselves were beginning to prove troublesome.

The commissioning of Leicester Square Regulating Room, which centralised much control of signalling, allowed a large number of traditional cabins on the line to be closed. LT Museum

The 1938 stock had never been the most trouble-free although it had given excellent service. By the end of the 1960s thought was being given to its replacement. Ordinarily, the Northern could have expected a completely new fleet of trains, but plans were now afoot to extend the Piccadilly Line to Heathrow Airport, justifying a new fleet for that line whose trains were then only a few years old. The planned move entailed the 1959 stock (with the few units of 1956 and 1962 origin as well) transferring to the Northern with thirty 1938 stock trains being thoroughly refurbished to remain in service to make up the shortfall.

There were worries about the 1938 stock conversions as rehabilitation had always proved both costly and unsuccessful in the past and it was with some relief that London Transport received sanction from its new owners, the Greater London Council, in 1970, to order new trains to top up the anticipated 1959 stock shortfall. There is some thought that another motive for this order was to support Metro-Cammell, then the sole surviving supplier of trains to the Underground, until the next generation of trains was ordered. However good the motives for the order, there was no time to design a new train and the 1972 stock became a re-hash of Victoria Line trains, warts and all, hastily adapted for two-person operation and even using some shunting control components from scrapped 1938 stock. New trains were obviously welcome, but they were in some ways ill-fitted for the purpose. They were uncomfortable for passengers and have never achieved particularly high levels of reliability.

Pending the transfer from the Piccadilly Line, authorisation of the then Fleet Line (now the Jubilee) in 1971 gave an opportunity to make further inroads into the ageing 1938 stock fleet, through the early purchase of its first batch of trains – 1972 MkII – for temporary use of the Northern. For a while over half the fleet was of modern trains, but from 1975 onwards 1959 type trains began to transfer in, giving the line problems of having three distinct stocks for a while. As the 1959 transfers gathered momentum, the Piccadilly Line management publicly referred to the situation and forecast that with the 'nearly new' trains, many of which were now actually at half-life, problems on the Northern would soon be over. It did not work; staff and passengers alike did not perceive 1959 stock as 'nearly new' and claimed that the Northern had been palmed off with another line's castoffs.

With a reversing loop, the Northern is one of the lines which, at any given time, has trains both the 'right' and 'wrong' way round. As the two cannot couple to each other, there is already a loss of flexibility. With two stocks this problem is magnified and has led to trains being cancelled through a lack of serviceable trains. The proportions of 1972 and 1959 stock trains rose and fell as policies changed, but ultimately less than 25% of the fleet was left as 1972 stock, some having been converted for use on the Victoria Line, and all of the MkII fleet working on the Bakerloo.

The period was not without a few major changes for the line. The construction of the Victoria Line led to the permanent closure of the Northern City Line between Drayton Park and Finsbury Park in October 1964. For the same reason Euston station was rebuilt, the City branch losing its island platform and gaining a new northbound running tunnel and platform. When this opened in October 1967 it was hailed as a preview of the new Victoria Line style. This move completed major changes at Euston, which had received a new ticket hall and lost its lift access as part of the reconstruction of the main line station in the early 1960s. In the same period both Old Street and London Bridge stations had undergone major reconstruction and were among the first examples of the post-war rekindling of the improvement of facilities at existing central area stations. Shortly afterwards a start was made on a major programme to replace the original lift equipment

For 35 years the 1938 stock was the mainstay of the Northern Line. By the late 1960s however, its increasing age and maintenance requirements, especially when compared with newer rolling stock, had made it costly to operate and thought was given to replacement. A southbound 1938 stock train is seen at Woodside Park. John Glover

The 1959 stock which was used to assist in the replacement of the Northern Line's 1938 stock owed much to its predecessor's classic design. A train is seen at Euston, City branch, where the station tunnel housed two tracks and an island platform until a new northbound tunnel was built in the mid-1960s. Capital Transport

at those stations where conversion to escalator operation could not be justified. By the mid-1980s Mornington Crescent was the only station on the Northern to depend solely on its original 1907 lifts, which lasted until August 1990.

Reconstruction work was also necessary on the bridges on the Barnet branch at this time: all were a hundred years old and becoming a liability. Perhaps the most attractive was at Argyle Road, Finchley, which in 1967 became the Underground's first pre-stressed concrete underline bridge. Another 'first' was a bridge of welded box girder construction, rolled into position in April 1970 to carry the railway over the Great North Road at Barnet. This bridge, which had a much longer span than the original, had to be welded on site in conditions designed to be as close as possible to the workshop to ensure consistent quality.

The last major change to the line was the withdrawal of the services on the Northern City Line on 4th October 1975 in preparation for its adoption by British Rail as part of the Great Northern suburban electrification scheme. Ten months later, the first main-line trains rumbled through. In February 1975 this little line had seen the Underground's worst peacetime disaster when a morning peak train passed through Moorgate station without stopping and crashed into the end of the tunnel: 42 people lost their lives. Following this incident all terminal stations on the Underground were provided with protection to prevent a buffer stop collision at any significant speed.

Through the years, the pattern of services had changed, particularly reflecting changing demand and a loss of evening and weekend traffic. In 1950, to effect economies, the pre-war practice of running shorter trains in the off-peak period was resumed so that

Between 1969 and 1976 centralised control was transferred to Cobourg Street, near Euston, to a purpose-built control room shared with the Victoria Line. All the remaining signal cabins (except Park Junction used for some shunting moves at Highgate depot) were closed. LUL

during the middle of the day trains had only three or four cars. Although this reduced mileage (and thus maintenance) and energy, it was costly in staff resources and there could be problems in re-forming long trains for the evening peak. The practice ended again after ten years, much simplifying the line's schedules. In 1965 the Northern lost another idiosyncrasy, in that for the first time Edgware branch trains stopped regularly at Mornington Crescent. Hitherto they had rumbled through without pausing, leaving Barnet services to collect the waiting few.

From 1982 onwards, the gentle decline in traffic was transformed into a very vigorous increase: in 1987 more people were carried than ever before, and the Northern carried nearly 700,000 passengers each day.

This upsurge, which took most by surprise, led to a completely unpredicted event. The ordering of a second batch of new trains for the Jubilee Line had brought the promise of a cascade of trains around the network, giving the Northern additional 1959 stock (from the Bakerloo Line). Rather than wait for these, it was decided to renovate five withdrawn trains of 1938 stock for operation on the Northern Line. The first of these went into service in 1986, 8½ years after the 'last' one had run on the Northern and nearly a year after withdrawal from the Bakerloo. Amongst the rather bland trains then running, these veterans were actually quite popular and it was in some ways a shame that enough 1959 trains had been released from the Bakerloo for us to say a second farewell to the red trains in spring 1988. The 1938 stock was not finished; units were sold to British Rail for use on the Isle of Wight to replace an earlier generation of trains, a few of which had started work on the Northern Line in 1923.

The deep level shelters built during the Second World War in anticipation of an unfulfilled express tube along the route of the Northern Line have found use by companies offering secure storage. The surface building for the one at Camden Town is illustrated here.

Strand booking hall. Passimeter booking offices were originally introduced to help speed passenger flows. As demand increased they were supplemented with automatic ticket machines issuing the most-requested single tickets. Increasingly however, the Edwardian surroundings, spartan at the outset, were showing signs of age, were becoming too cluttered and were in need of a face-lift. Strand was closed for reconstruction in 1973 and re-opened as part of a new Charing Cross Underground station with the Jubilee Line in 1979.

LT Museum/LUL/
Capital Transport

The Northern Today and Tomorrow

In the six years up to end of the 1980s demand for Underground services had risen by nearly 70%, a surge without precedent anywhere in the world. The Northern now carries 720,000 passengers per day, more than ever before, on a railway which has seen under-investment for decades. Signalling has been reduced in capacity to match the once-declining demand and is lacking the refined control necessary for intensive services on a complex system. The trains are ageing and the stations reeling from escalator problems arising from past economies in maintenance and inadequate design of those installed in the post-war decades.

The line serves some of the most important and influential areas of London, but it still has a poor public image: the 'Misery Line' tag is still dusted down, especially by the less responsible press anxious to stir scandal and sell more papers, despite the vast improvements on the line since the name was coined. Perhaps the general feeling is best summed up by a London Broadcasting Company (LBC) radio journalist who dismissed the line as 'notoriously antiquated'. Not true, but popular belief.

In November 1987 a tragic fire occurred at King's Cross, having started part way up an escalator shaft, which was to be a major watershed in the Underground's development. Thirty-two people lost their lives in the event which most people familiar with the Underground had believed could not happen. The immediate effect for the Northern was the closure of its platforms at King's Cross until February 1989 while the escalators were replaced. The inquiry that followed found that there was an underlying weakness in senior management: the scene was set for a fundamental change of direction.

At Edgware a new bus station has been built behind the Underground station, in conjunction with the Broadwalk Shopping Centre development. The rebuilt station forecourt includes a colonnade of five commercial units in the style of the original station. R.E. Bayman

Today's drive for improvement started in November 1988 with a fundamental change in management practice, turning each line into a business unit headed by a General Manager, instead of the former concept of Divisions responsible solely for operational supervision. Decision making, authority and responsibility were to be devolved from the remote head office, to local managers, who had the benefit of being closer to the customer. This move generated tremendous enthusiasm amongst local managers, much of which began to rub off onto staff, without which it is doubtful whether the railway would have survived soaring increases in safety standards without having to endure temporary closures. With this spirit the Underground is becoming the world's first railway to take on a safety management system to recognisable international standards. Alongside this go higher training standards, including the provision of regular refresher training to ensure that staff are prepared for any eventuality. It is recognised that this can be achieved only through effective teamwork, with commitment to safety and service through all levels and functions of the organisation.

Much of the early work of the new organisation had to be devoted to 'behind the scenes' changes, but as the Northern neared its centenary some changes were becoming visible. On stations, work has begun on the provision of improved security and safety, with new alarm systems and the removal of materials – such as laminated panelling – once considered adequately fire safe but now regarded as an unnecessary hazard. This had led to many stations reaching the status of perpetual building sites, but the majority of passengers are prepared to endure temporary difficulty for long-term improvement.

Amongst the more controversial innovations of the later 1980s was the implementation of the Underground Ticketing System (UTS). The self-service ticket machines went down quite well but the ticket gates caused much initial emotion until people got used to them, and found that the throughput of a batch of gates was a lot greater than conventional ticket barriers.

Slightly earlier the Northern had benefited from two major improvements in the provision of information. Visually, dot-matrix train indicators were provided on most platforms to provide estimated arrival times for the next three trains. The Northern was the first line to receive this equipment, but there were many teething problems, not least the famous tendency for a minute to equal 84 seconds, which needed addressing. Hardware capacity was dealt with early in the system's life, but a programme of changes to software and communications was developed for implementation in 1991.

Parallel improvements in audible information on stations came with the development of a comprehensive centralised public address system, although again by the end of the 1980s some fundamental design faults were becoming evident. Despite these problems, the passenger in 1989 was much better informed of what was happening than at any time in the railway's history.

The south end of the line had developed an unenviable reputation for crime. Although absolute figures were not high when compared with street crime there was no doubt that the area around Tooting and Clapham had the highest crime rates of the Underground. In 1985 the policing of the area was increased and a number of closed circuit television (CCTV) cameras installed. Over the following two years this had the effect of halving assaults and pickpocketing. In 1987 it was decided to intensify the campaign. Staff at six stations in the area were increased and became more visible, so-called 'focal points' were established, where a supervisor could see what was going on and be seen by the customer, who now had an information facility as well. From the focal point staff could monitor virtually all parts of the station by CCTV and there was continuous recording of the output of all cameras. Passengers anywhere on the station

At six stations at the south end of the line, Station Focal Points have been created. These highly visible rooms for staff also house television monitors and video-recording facilities and are linked to remote help points in all parts of the station. Used normally for information, the deterrent value of the facilities has helped considerably in cutting crime rates.

were within easy reach of a 'help point' which could be used either to obtain information or to raise the alarm in the event of emergency. Any emergency call not answered promptly by local staff was passed straight through to the Police Information Room.

The further success of this scheme was considerable. It benefited from a dedicated team of staff and from warm co-operation between the staff and the local police officers. A programme of 'surgeries', where staff and police would meet passengers, was started with excellent feedback from all concerned. Crime rates fell still further; there was even some evidence that evening traffic, always the most threatened, was increasing again. The way was clear for the scheme to be extended to other stations, ultimately across the Underground.

Other improvements also began to bite. Cleaning standards were increased at nearly all stations, to the extent that passengers actually started to comment on them. This was matched by intensive cleaning of the trains themselves – initially behind the scenes to remove potentially flammable accumulations – and then through the saloons. Again, favourable comment was forthcoming. The changes were helped during autumn 1989 by the replacement of the trains' old brake blocks by new materials which wore much more slowly and thus deposited far less dust (a reduction of 60%), coupled with a resumption of regular cleaning of station fluorescent lighting tubes abandoned some years earlier. The result was clearly visible. In November 1989 the campaign was rounded off by the initiation of litter removal from trains during the day at the main termini. The immediate result was collection of 15-20 sacks of rubbish daily, which hitherto had been carried about the line all day – unsightly and hazardous mess. The perceived need, following the King's Cross fire, to call the fire brigade to any suspected incident, however small (even the mildest smell of smoke) became very disruptive from 1988, given the brigade's duty to be satisfied that any fire was out. Over the years the Northern's tunnels had become ingrained with generations of dust and grease – never in great accumulation, but given that most tunnels had seen two or three hundred trains pass each day, every day for decades, some deposit was inevitable. It is very easy for a stray spark from a collector shoe to ignite this deposit, or litter, and start a small fire. For this reason, litter removal in tunnels was stepped up during 1989 and this was followed by the start of an intensive and laborious cleaning of the trackside, including the ballast laid between the rails, a programme which could last for years.

Efforts were also needed on the trains to go beyond cleaning regimes and provide interiors which could take full advantage of the fire-safe materials now available, whilst at the same time giving a brighter and more comfortable ride. Contracts were placed early in 1990 for the complete refurbishment of interiors on three stocks, including the Northern's 1972 stock trains, on which work is due to get under way in spring 1992. Although the earlier 1959 stock has insufficient life left to justify a complete refit, work started in 1989 on replacing ceilings and installing public address and passenger alarm facilities, to bring them into line with current safety expectations. As trains are overhauled they are also being given brighter interiors and graffiti-resistant paints to provide a reasonable appearance for the remaining years.

Facing Page **Brighter interiors are being introduced on the Northern Line's 1959 stock trains to replace the original grey colour scheme. One of the first to be treated is illustrated; later ones are receiving brighter seat covering also.** Capital Transport

Above **The current interior of 1972 stock reflects the design styles of the 1960s, being based on the 1967 Victoria Line stock. Although functional, by today's standards it is not attractive. Refurbishment of the stock is planned and the prototype car layout reflects the needs of all types of passenger, especially those disabled. Brighter colours with modern durable materials are used and communication facilities are improved.** R.E. Bayman

Below **Externally the unpainted aluminium will disappear and a new livery will be carried. Modern paint technology enables a lightweight highly durable paint to be applied, which is easy to clean and defeats the efforts of those who would deface it with graffiti.** LUL

Major improvements to the train service are hindered by the complexity of the line's junctions and the limitations of the signalling control system. Some of the line's bottlenecks can, however, be eased by minor signalling revisions and changes to working practice. Plans are being drawn up to implement some of these changes between 1992 and 1995 and, using trains displaced by new stock on the Central Line, to modestly increase frequencies in areas where overcrowding is a problem. However, the relief expected from these schemes is unlikely to take the line through the 1990s with enough capacity improvement for the next century. As the Northern enters its second hundred years very much more spectacular changes are being planned.

There are a number of reasons for these changes. It is clear that the line needs to achieve better regularity and reliability than it can with existing infrastructure to meet even today's demand. Usage of public transport is increasing throughout London, however, and in this light the Northern is incapable of contributing adequately towards the Capital's transport needs. With new signalling and trains it can increase its capacity by 30% in some areas, making full use of the currently under-utilised (and highly expensive) track and tunnels. This would justify change by itself: in practice the City branch of the Northern can expect some exceptional demand increases during the closing decade of this century. The line will connect with both the Jubilee Line and the Docklands Light Railway serving London's new Docklands. It also serves the areas both north and south of the Square Mile which offer an explosion in office developments, and the intended development north of King's Cross (both at King's Cross Station itself and at Mornington Crescent). The King's Cross site would also include the major international terminal for cross-Channel traffic.

In a few years, London Bridge station will become an interchange between the Northern and Jubilee Lines. To cater for this on top of an already increased demand, substantial new works are to be carried out including a new platform-level concourse and a new ticket hall.

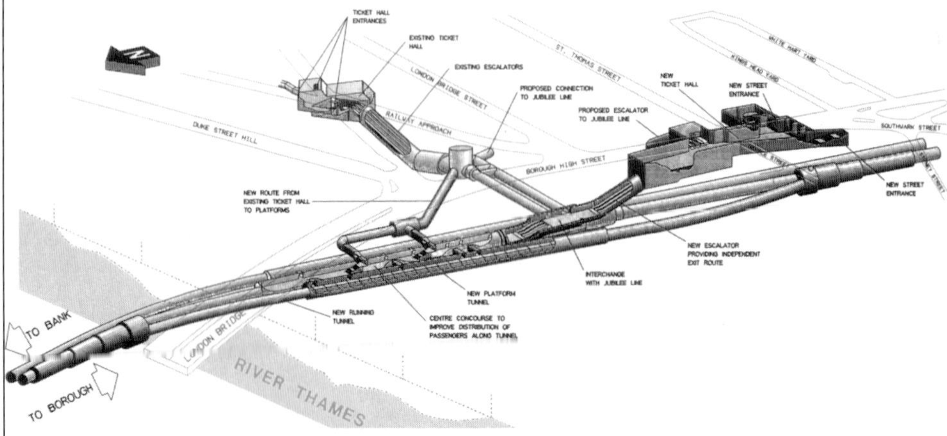

LONDON BRIDGE
NORTHERN LINE SCHEME FOR CONGESTION RELIEF

One of the biggest traffic growths on the Northern Line has been at Angel station. Over the years the usage of the area surrounding the station has changed significantly and now there are a large number of high-density offices nearby. The original island platform built in 1900 no longer adequately meets passenger demand at peak times. Authority to completely rebuild the station has been obtained and a new length of running tunnel with a new platform will be built. The existing platform will be extended over the redundant track. The artist's sketches show the new concourse and the new station entrance. LUL

Work at Bank station to incorporate the Docklands Light Railway will also improve Northern Line facilities, with new direct subway links throughout the station and improved interchange. DLR

A key improvement at busy stations such as Tottenham Court Road is the provision of a modern Station Control Room. The supervisor observes all parts of the station through television monitors, is informed of equipment status by visual indications on the desk and has direct radio communication with the station staff, with other resources a telephone call away. LUL

An improvement much appreciated by passengers has been the softening of stations with shrubs and flowers. This colourful display is at Morden station. R.E. Bayman

Current proposals for 1995 Stock envisage six-car trains operating, made up of two three-car units, similar in length to the 1973 Stock on the Piccadilly Line. Trains would be automatically operated but with a driver in the leading cab, and would have improved acceleration and braking. LUL

Internally the 1995 Stock would take advantage of new bogie designs, which, with small wheels, allow the whole of the bogie to be located underneath the floor. Consequently, for the first time on London's tube railways, the internal design can be based entirely around passenger flows inside the carriage. LUL

The demands expected of the year 2000 can be met only with totally new equipment, both trainborne and lineside. The trains themselves, being developed as the City & South London passes its centenary, will be designed specifically to obtain the optimum capacity for the line, given the need to cope with the line's short platforms and steep gradients; together with the conflicting needs of short distance inner-city passengers and those travelling from the green belt suburbs to the north and south. Gangways will be more spacious though without sacrificing comfortable seating arrangements, and doors arranged to suit passenger flow rather than engineering needs. Ventilation will be improved and audible and visual information will be provided about the location of the train. Although the trains will be safer than any so far, the emergency evacuation facilities will also be improved to bring new standards to the Underground.

The trains are only part of the improvements. Systems now exist which can allow trains to operate significantly more closely together than under conventional signalling régimes, and with even greater safety. They also allow much more intensive supervision of progress than possible hitherto, so that trains can be accurately adjusted to arrive when intended, avoiding uncomfortable waits between stations. So far, none of these systems has been used on a deep-level tube, nor on any railway as complex as the Northern, but testing was under way in mid-1990 to establish the benefits of rival technologies to take the Northern into the 21st Century.

Although increased efficiency will in itself provide more capacity, up to 10% more trains will also be needed and these will require completely different facilities compared with those now available, which were built between Edwardian times and the 1920s. Studies are now under way into the support facilities needed for tomorrow's Northern, which may result in an alternative being proposed to the cramped workshop conditions at Golders Green, as well as new sidings to cope with extra trains.

The greater throughput of passengers requires comparable improvements to handling capacity at stations. By the beginning of 1990 work was under way for a totally new station at Angel, and schemes were in Parliament for very major extensions to London Bridge and Tottenham Court Road stations. Each of these will have interchange with new lines if current plans come to fruition: London Bridge with the Jubilee Line and Tottenham Court Road with the Chelsea-Hackney Line and East-West Crossrail, which would see new entrances opened through much of north eastern Soho. Major capacity increases are also being considered for Camden Town, Old Street, Clapham North and Clapham Common, the last two being the only remaining narrow island platform stations of the old City & South London pattern after the rebuilding of Angel. In the suburbs the replacement of the existing and inadequate facilities is under investigation at both Golders Green and Finchley Central: at the latter this could yet see a grand new station on the lines intended before the war.

Through all these changes it is intended that the pattern of services will remain very much as today. Certainly, it would be possible to overcome some of today's problems by splitting services and forming two lines (today's depot provision dictates that these would be Edgware–Charing Cross–Kennington and Barnet/Mill Hill–City–Morden). This solution is hardly practicable, though, since a number of stations would require enhancement amounting in cost to tens of millions of pounds to cope with extra interchange traffic. The line would be left with inferior options for its customers and none of the operational flexibility which serves it so well when disruption takes place. Nevertheless, the splitting of the line in two must remain an option for the late 1990s if the line does not benefit from the major investment it needs to take it into the 21st Century.